D0818151

Hands-On Mobile
App Testing

Hands-On Mobile App Testing

A Guide for Mobile Testers and Anyone Involved in the Mobile App Business

Daniel Knott

♦♦Addison-Wesley

New York • Boston • Indianapolis • San Francisco
Toronto • Montreal • London • Munich • Paris • Madrid
Capetown • Sydney • Tokyo • Singapore • Mexico City

Many of the designations used by manufacturers and sellers to distinguish their products are claimed as trademarks. Where those designations appear in this book, and the publisher was aware of a trademark claim, the designations have been printed with initial capital letters or in all capitals.

The author and publisher have taken care in the preparation of this book, but make no expressed or implied warranty of any kind and assume no responsibility for errors or omissions. No liability is assumed for incidental or consequential damages in connection with or arising out of the use of the information or programs contained herein.

For information about buying this title in bulk quantities, or for special sales opportunities (which may include electronic versions; custom cover designs; and content particular to your business, training goals, marketing focus, or branding interests), please contact our corporate sales department at corpsales@pearsoned.com or (800) 382-3419.

For government sales inquiries, please contact governmentsales@pearsoned.com.

For questions about sales outside the U.S., please contact international@pearsoned.com.

Visit us on the Web: informit.com/aw

Library of Congress Cataloging-in-Publication Data
Knott, Daniel.
  Hands-on mobile app testing : a guide for mobile testers and anyone involved in the mobile app business / Daniel Knott.
      pages   cm
  Includes index.
  ISBN 978-0-13-419171-3 (pbk. : alk. paper)—ISBN 0-13-419171-4
  1. Mobile apps—Testing. I. Title.
  QA76.76.T48K64 2015
  006.3—dc23

                                                                2015009688

ISBN-13: 978-0-13-419171-3
ISBN-10: 0-13-419171-4

Text printed in the United States on recycled paper at RR Donnelley in Crawfordsville, Indiana.
First printing, May 2015

*For my wife, Sarah. Thank you
very much for your support and
encouragement while I wrote this book.*

Contents

Preface

Mobile phones have been around since the middle of the 1970s. The devices have of course changed profoundly since then, but the biggest change came in 2007 when Apple presented its first iPhone. From that moment on, the mobile smartphone market has known only one direction—UP! Eight years later, touch devices such as smartphones and tablets have become ubiquitous. More than two million apps are available for download in the stores of the biggest vendors, and this number is still rising.[1] There are apps for every aspect of our lives, ranging from photos and music, to office applications and games, and on to fitness and health. But what about the quality of those apps? Are they reliable, trustworthy, easy to use, well developed, and tested?

This book is a practical guide to mobile testing for anyone who works in the mobile business, but it is especially aimed at mobile testers.

Why I Wrote This Book

It all started in 2010 when I had the opportunity to work on my first mobile project. The mobile team I worked in was responsible for developing a mobile Web app, a native Android app, and a native iOS app. This was the company's first mobile project and a completely new testing environment for the quality assurance department. Together with a colleague, I had the chance to build a mobile testing strategy from scratch. We evaluated several test automation tools to see which one fit best in our software development lifecycle. At that time, mobile testing tools were few and far between, and at a very early development stage. We then tried several testing approaches and tools. Of course we failed with some of them, but in the end the whole team, the company, and our customers were happy.

Another reason why I wrote this book was because of my blog, www.adventuresinqa.com. I started blogging in 2011 after giving a presentation at the Agile

---

1. iOS Store numbers, www.engadget.com/2014/06/02/apples-wwdc-2014-in-numbers-40-million-on-mavericks-and-more/; Android Play Store numbers, www.appbrain.com/stats/number-of-android-apps. Numbers are from June 2014.

Testing Days in Potsdam, Germany. This was my first talk at a major testing conference, and I was the only speaker on the agenda who spoke about mobile testing. After my presentation I was very busy for the rest of the conference as a lot of people approached me to ask about mobile testing, the approaches I use, what kind of tools I use, and so forth. The huge interest in and the lack of knowledge about mobile testing convinced me to start writing a blog. The goal was to share my knowledge of mobile testing and to exchange views and ideas with other mobile testers, while also improving my written English skills. So far I've written about 90 posts covering mobile apps and testing, and I never expected so many people from around the world to take an interest in my blog. The feedback I've gotten so far has been great, and it convinced me to take the next step.

That step is what you're reading: a book about mobile testing that captures my practical experience and knowledge for anyone involved in the mobile business. I hope you enjoy reading this book and can learn something new about the mobile testing business.

Who Should Read This Book?

This book is aimed at anyone who is interested in mobile apps and mobile testing, ranging from junior to expert mobile testers who are already involved in mobile development teams.

This book is also ideal for software test managers who need to manage mobile testing teams or to select a mobile test strategy. It's also great for software testers who are new to this topic and want to switch to mobile technologies.

Software developers who want to know more about mobile testing and testing their mobile apps have also come to the right place.

This book is also intended for product managers looking to gain further insights into the challenging job of mobile testing.

Topics Covered in This Book

This book contains the following chapters:

- **Chapter 1: What's Special about Mobile Testing?** The first chapter focuses on the special characteristics of mobile testing. It provides an introduction to mobile user expectations, mobile data networks, mobile devices, and why mobile testing is software testing.

- **Chapter 2: Introduction to Mobile Devices and Apps** Chapter 2 introduces mobile data networks and what is important to know about them.

The chapter also describes the mobile device evolution from dumb phones to the current smartphones. Furthermore, this chapter introduces the different types of apps and possible app business models.

- **Chapter 3: Challenges in Mobile Testing**   Chapter 3 is all about mobile testing challenges and how to handle them. There are challenges such as the customer, device fragmentation, sensors and interfaces, system apps, and mobile browsers. Each section of the chapter provides solutions for handling those challenges in your daily business as a mobile tester.

- **Chapter 4: How to Test Mobile Apps**   Chapter 4 is all about how to test mobile applications. This chapter explains the differences among emulators, simulators, and real devices. It also explains where to test a mobile app. Furthermore, this chapter provides several functional and nonfunctional approaches to testing a mobile app. In addition, this chapter presents mobile testing mind maps, mnemonics, and checklists to improve your mobile testing efforts.

- **Chapter 5: Mobile Test Automation and Tools**   Chapter 5 covers the topic of mobile test automation, which is a very important one. The chapter introduces the different test automation tool types and approaches. It provides ideas for how to select the right mobile test automation tool for your test environment. Additionally, the chapter provides an overview of the current state of mobile test automation tools for Android and iOS.

- **Chapter 6: Additional Mobile Testing Methods**   Chapter 6 provides an overview of additional mobile testing methods such as crowd and cloud testing. Both methods are explained, including the pros and cons and where it makes sense to use them in your mobile testing approach.

- **Chapter 7: Mobile Test and Launch Strategies**   Chapter 7 deals with the topic of mobile test and launch strategies. It is very important for developers of mobile apps to have both in place in order to develop, test, and launch a mobile app with high quality. This chapter provides lots of ideas about and examples of how to establish mobile test and launch strategies.

- **Chapter 8: Important Skills for Mobile Testers**   Chapter 8 describes the required skill set of a mobile tester. Furthermore, the chapter provides ideas and solutions on how to improve the skills of a mobile tester.

- **Chapter 9: What's Next? And Final Thoughts**   Chapter 9 is the final chapter of this book and deals with possible topics that software testers may have to handle in the near future. The chapter contains topics such as the Internet of Things, connected homes, connected cars, and wearables. At the end, five key success factors are provided.

Each chapter focuses on the practical side of mobile testing. Sure, there will be some theoretical parts, but most of the content is based on real-life experience as a mobile tester.

How to Use This Book

This book is a practical guide to mobile testing. You can read it from front to back to get an overview of mobile testing, or you can jump straight to the chapters you're most interested in. There's one important piece of advice you should bear in mind while reading this book: make sure you have at least one mobile device next to you so you can try out the things you read.

If you want to get started with the test automation tools mentioned in this book, now would be a good time to get your computer.

Acknowledgments

Thanks to Tobias Geyer for being my dedicated reviewer. Without your contribution, encouragement, help, feedback, and critical questions this book would not have become what it is.

Thanks to Dominik Dary for your awesome feedback on mobile test automation and helping me shape the content of several chapters in this book.

Thanks to Rudolf Grötz for your great ideas about several graphics and images. Thank you very much for your help and contribution to the crowd and cloud testing chapter.

Thanks to Dagmar Mathes who gave me the opportunity to be part of the mobile testing business. Thanks for your trust, support, and encouragement.

Thanks to Sergej Mudruk and Christoph Wielgus for your support in reading my book and providing me with very useful feedback.

Thanks to Andrew Rennison for being my great copy editor, for your help and constant contribution to my text.

And last but not least, I want to say thank you to all software testers out there for sharing your knowledge of various software testing and mobile testing topics. Thanks for your contribution to the community and all of the time and effort you put in.

About the Author

Daniel Knott has been working in the field of software development and software testing since 2003. He started his career as a trainee at IBM where he was involved in enterprise software development and testing.

After his time at IBM, Daniel studied computer science at the University of Applied Sciences in Wiesbaden, Germany. Software testing became a passion during his time at university and is the reason he chose a career in the field. Daniel has worked at several companies in various industries where he was responsible for testing Web, desktop, and mobile applications. During a number of projects he developed fully automated testing frameworks for Android, iOS, and Web applications. Daniel is a well-known mobile expert, a speaker at various conferences in Europe, and a blog author (www.adventuresinqa.com).

Furthermore, Daniel is the founder and organizer of two local software testing user groups in central Germany. One is the Software Test User Group Rhein Main (www.stugrm.de) and the other is the Rhein Main Mobile Quality Crew (www.meetup.com/Rhein-Main-Mobile-Quality-Crew).

Chapter 1

What's Special about Mobile Testing?

Before I start describing the unique aspects of mobile testing, I'd like to share a true story with you.

What's special about mobile testing? Someone asked me this exact question several years ago while at a testing conference. I started talking about mobile technologies, apps, how to test them, and what's special about mobile testing. The guy simply smiled at me and said, "But it's software just on a smaller screen. There's nothing special about it." He was really arrogant and didn't see the challenges presented by mobile testing. No matter which arguments I used to convince him, he didn't believe in the importance of mobile technologies, apps, and testing.

I met the same guy again in 2014 while at a testing conference where he talked about mobile testing. He spoke about the importance of apps and how important it is to test them.

As you can see, it's very easy to underestimate new technologies. As a software tester it's especially helpful to be curious about learning something new and exploring new technologies to broaden your skills.

So let's come back to the initial question: What's special about mobile testing? I think I can assume you have at least one mobile device, namely, a smartphone. Or maybe you have a tablet, or even both. If you look at your device(s), what do you see? Just a small computer with little shiny icons on its screen? Or do you see a very personal computer with lots of sensors and input options that contains all of your private data? Please take a minute to think about that.

My smartphone and tablet are very personal computers that hold almost all of my data, be it e-mails, SMS, photos, music, videos, and the like. I can access my data no matter where I am and use my smartphone as a navigation and information system to find out more about my surroundings. For that reason I expect my apps to be reliable, fast, and easy to use.

In those three sentences I described my personal expectations of mobile devices and apps. But you may have entirely different expectations, as does the next person. And this brings me to the first special characteristic or unique aspect of mobile testing: user expectations.

User Expectations

In my opinion, the user of an app is the main focus and main challenge for mobile teams. The fact that every user has unique expectations makes it difficult to develop and deliver the "right" app to customers. As several reports and surveys have shown, mobile users have far higher expectations of mobile apps than of other software such as browser applications.[1] The majority of reports and surveys state that nearly 80% of users delete an app after using it for the first time! The top four reasons for deletion are always bad design, poor usability, slow loading time, and crashes immediately after installation. Nearly 60% of users will delete an app that requires registration, and more than half of users expect an app to launch in under two seconds. If the app takes more time, it gets deleted. Again, more than half of users experience crashes the very first time they start an app. An average user checks his or her mobile device every six minutes and has around 40 apps installed. Based on those numbers, you can deduce that mobile users have really high expectations when it comes to usability, performance, and reliability. Those three characteristics were mentioned most often by far when users were asked about their experience with mobile apps.

Currently there are more than two million apps available in the app stores of the biggest vendors. A lot of apps perform the same task, meaning that there's always at least one competitor app, which makes it very easy for consumers to download a different app as it's just a single tap away. Here are some points you should keep in mind when developing and testing a mobile app:

- Gather information about your possible target customer group.
- Ask your customers about their needs.
- Your app needs to solve a problem for the user.
- Usability is really important.

---

1. http://offers2.compuware.com/rs/compuware/images/Mobile_App_Survey_Report.pdf

- Your app needs to be reliable and robust.
- App performance is really important.
- Apps need to be beautiful.

There are, of course, a plethora of other things you should take into account, but if you pay attention to these points, your users are likely to be happy.

You've probably already heard of the KISS principle.[2] KISS is an acronym for Keep It Simple, Stupid and is always a useful reminder—especially for software projects—to not inflate the software with just another function or option. Keeping it small, easy, and simple is best in most cases and is likely to make your customers happy. Inspired by KISS, I came up with my own principle for mobile apps: KIFSU (see Figure 1.1). This abbreviation is a good mnemonic to help you cover customer needs and a constant reminder not to inflate apps with useless functions.

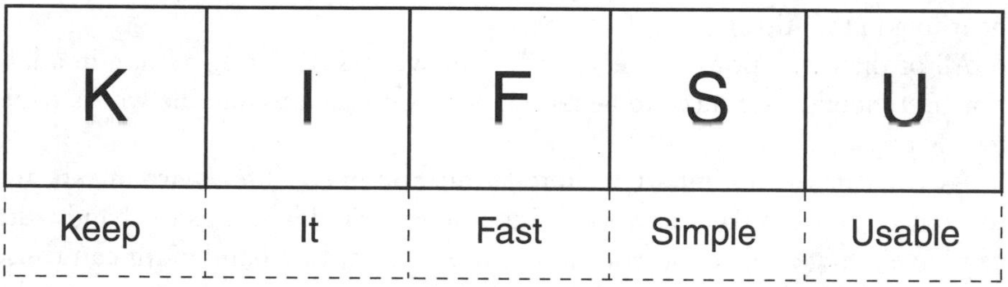

K	I	F	S	U
Keep	It	Fast	Simple	Usable

Figure 1.1 *KIFSU*

Mobility and Data Networks

Another challenge mobile apps have to deal with more than software running on computers is the fact that users are moving around while they use apps, which often requires an Internet connection to fetch data from the backend and serve the user with updates and information.

Mobile apps need to be tested in real life, in real environments where the potential user will use them. For example, if you're testing an app for snowboarders and skiers that accesses slope information, one that is able to record the speed of the current downhill run and makes it possible for users to share records directly with their friends, you need to test these functions on a slope. Otherwise you can't guarantee that every feature will work as expected.

---

2. http://people.apache.org/~fhanik/kiss.html

Of course, there are parts of an app that you can test in a lab situation, such as slope information availability or whether or not the app can be installed, but what about recording a person's speed, the weather conditions, or the Internet connection at the top of a mountain?

The weather conditions on a mountain, in particular, can be very difficult to handle as they can, of course, range from sunshine to a snowstorm. In such scenarios you will probably find lots of bugs regarding the usability and design of an app. Maybe you'll also find some functional bugs due to the temperature, which may have an impact on your hardware and, in turn, your app.

As I already mentioned, the speed and availability of Internet connections could vary in such regions. You will probably have a good network connection with high speed at the top of the mountain and a really poor one down in the valley. What happens if you have a bad or no Internet connection while using the app? Will it crash or will it still work? What happens if the mobile device changes network providers while the app is being used? (This is a common scenario when using apps close to an international border, such as when snowboarding in the Alps.)

All of these questions are very hard to answer when testing an app in a lab. You as a mobile tester need to be mobile and connected to data networks while testing apps.

As you can see, it's important to test your app in real-life environments and to carry out tests in data networks with different bandwidths as the bandwidth can have a huge impact on your app; for example, low bandwidth can cause unexpected error messages, and the switch between high and low bandwidth can cause performance issues or freezes.

Here's an exercise for you. Take any app you want and find three usage scenarios where the environment and/or network connection could cause problems.

Mobile Devices

Before you continue reading, pick up your mobile device and look at it. Take your device in your hand and look at every side of it without turning it on. What do you see?

You will most likely see a device with a touch-sensitive screen, a device with several hardware buttons with a charger, a headphone connection, and a camera. That's probably it—you're not likely to have more than five hardware buttons (except for smartphones with a physical keyboard).

In an era when the words *cell phone* have become synonymous with smartphone, it's important to remember that there used to be other types of cell phones, so-called dumb phones and feature phones that have lots more hardware buttons for making a call or typing a message. With a conventional dumb phone you are only able to make a call, type a message, or store a contact list; they're not usually connected to the Internet. The more advanced ones, the feature phones, have games, a calendar, or a very basic Web browser with the option to connect to the Internet. But all these phones are really basic in terms of functionality and expandability as users aren't able to install apps or easily update the software to a newer version, if it all. Both types of phones are still available, especially in emerging markets, but since 2013 more smartphones have been sold worldwide than dumb phones or feature phones,[3] and this trend is likely to continue as time goes on. In fact, in the next couple of years dumb phones and feature phones will be a thing of the past.

The phones we use nowadays are completely different from the "old" ones. Current smartphones are mini supercomputers with lots of functionality in terms of hardware and software. They're packed with various sensors such as brightness, proximity, acceleration, tilt, and much more. Besides that, all modern smartphones have both front- and rear-facing cameras, various communication interfaces such as Bluetooth, near field communication (NFC), and Global Positioning System (GPS), as well as Wi-Fi and cellular networks to connect to the Internet. Depending on the mobile platform and mobile manufacturer, you may find an array of other hardware features.

From a software point of view, smartphones offer lots of application programming interfaces (APIs) for manufacturers, developers, and users to extend smartphone capabilities with apps.

If you just focus on the major mobile platforms, iOS and Android, there are plenty of hardware and software combinations that mobile testers have to deal with. The fact that there are so many combinations is known as fragmentation. Mobile device fragmentation is a huge topic and yet another challenge when it comes to mobile testing.

You can't test your app with every possible hardware and software combination. And the fact that you should test your app in a real environment makes it even more impossible. Mobile testers need to find a strategy to downsize the effort of testing on different devices and to find a way to test on the right devices.

But how can that be accomplished? By testing on just one mobile platform? By testing on just the latest device? By testing with just the latest software version?

---

3. www.gartner.com/newsroom/id/2665715

Before you define a strategy, you should keep in mind that every app is unique, has unique requirements, has other problems to solve, and has a unique user base. With these points in mind, you can ask yourself the following questions to find the "right" mobile devices for testing:

- Who is my user base?
- How old is the average user?
- How many men or women are in my target user group?
- Which platform is used most among that user base?
- Which device is used most?
- Which software version is installed on most of the phones?
- What kind of sensors does my app use?
- How does the app communicate with the outside world?
- What is my app's main use case?

Of course, there are lots more questions to ask, but if you answer most of the ones I suggest, the list of possible devices you should consider testing is much shorter.

In later chapters I will describe other techniques for selecting the right devices for mobile testing.

Mobile Release Cycles

Now that you know how to find the right devices for testing your app, it doesn't mean that the process is over. To be honest, it's never going to end!

The main mobile manufacturers release a new flagship phone with more features every year. In and around those releases they bring out other phones for different user scenarios and user groups. This is especially true in the Android world where every new phone comes with a new version of the operating system packed with new features, designs, or APIs. There are multiple software releases within the course of a year, ranging from bug fixes to feature releases. You as a mobile tester need to be sure that your app will run on the latest hardware and software.

But how should you handle these situations? By buying every phone that appears on the market? By constantly updating to the latest operating system version?

Again, the most important factors are your target customer group and the app you're testing. When you know that your target group always uses the latest and fastest phones on the market, you need to buy those phones as soon as they appear. Regardless of whether or not your target group is up-to-date, you should always monitor the mobile market.

You need to know when the main vendors are due to release new flagship phones that a lot of people are likely to buy. You also need to know when the operating systems receive patches, new features, or new design patterns.

So the answer to the question of whether you need to buy every phone and constantly update the operating systems is yes and no. Of course you don't need to buy every phone that's on the market, but you should consider updating to the latest operating system version. When doing so, keep in mind that not every user will install the update. Many people don't know how to do that, or they don't care about new versions. You need at least some phones that are running older versions of the operating system to see how the app reacts in that environment. Older versions of the operating system are also needed to reproduce reported problems and bugs.

A good way to manage all this is to stick with the same operating system version on the phones that you have and buy new phones with the latest software version. This of course leads to another problem—it's really expensive! Not every manager wants to spend so much money on mobile devices when a phone is going to be used for only a couple of months. A solution for that is to rent devices. There are several providers and Open Device Labs where you can rent a device for a certain period of time (a list of providers can be found in Chapter 3, "Challenges in Mobile Testing"). Another way to rent devices is the mobile device cloud as there are a number of providers who give mobile testers exclusive access to the physical devices they have made available in the cloud. Just use your search engine and check them out.

In the mobile projects I've worked on, we always had the top ten to 15 devices used by our target user group in different variations for developing and testing. This was a good number of devices that covered nearly 90% of our target group. With those ten to 15 devices we were able to find most of the critical bugs; the remaining 10% of devices we didn't have were of no major consequence to the project or user expectations.

In order to handle the fast pace of mobile release cycles, you should keep the following things in mind:

- Monitor the mobile device and software market.
- Know when new phones will be rolled out.
- Find out about the new features of the operating systems.
- Keep an eye on your target customer group to see if new devices are showing up in your statistics.

- Think twice before updating a phone to the latest operating system version.

- Buy new phones with the latest operating system version.

- If buying is not an option, rent the devices.

Updating, buying, and maintaining all of your devices is a challenging task and should not be underestimated! At some point, depending on the number of test devices used within a project, this could be a full-time job.

Mobile Testing Is Software Testing

Let's come back to the story I told at the beginning of this chapter when the guy at the conference didn't believe in the importance of mobile testing. He had the attitude that mobile testing is not real software testing. In his opinion, mobile apps were only small programs with less functionality and no real challenges when it comes to software testing. But this is definitely not the case. If you look at the topics I described in this chapter, you should have an initial impression about the challenging job of a mobile tester. Mobile testing is totally different from testing software applications such as Web or desktop applications. With mobile apps, physical devices have far more influence over the software that is running on them when compared to other software such as Web applications. Because there are so many different smartphones available on the market, mobile testers need to focus a lot more on hardware during the testing process. In addition, users moving around and using different data networks force mobile testers to be on the move while testing.

Besides the hardware, user expectations play an important part in the daily business of a mobile tester and need to be taken seriously.

There are many more topics and issues mobile testers need to know about in order to help the whole team release a successful app. The rest of the chapters in this book will cover the following topics:

- More challenges for mobile testers and solutions to those challenges

- How to test mobile apps systematically

- How to select the right mobile test automation tool

- The different concepts of mobile test automation tools

- How to find the right mobile testing strategy

- Additional mobile testing methods

- Required skills for mobile testers

Keep the topics from this chapter in mind as a starting point. Keep your app simple and fast (remember KIFSU). Test while you're on the move, and test on different devices based on your target customer group.

Summary

The first chapter of this book mentioned some very important topics from the mobile testing world. As you have seen, mobile testing is completely different from testing on other technologies such as laptops or desktop computers. The biggest difference between mobile and other technologies is that the mobile user is on the move while he or she is using your product. Therefore, it is very important to know about the different data networks and the different types of mobile devices.

This chapter also provided a first overview of mobile users' high expectations. It is really important to keep KIFSU in mind when designing, developing, and testing a mobile app. It will help you to focus on the important elements and not waste time on unnecessary features that your users won't use.

And last but not least, this chapter should remind you to never underestimate a new technology. Be open-minded and curious to improve your daily work life.

Chapter 2

Introduction to Mobile Devices and Apps

Before I dive deeper into the testing chapters, I'd like to introduce you to the history of mobile devices and cellular networks. This may sound a bit boring, but as you will see by the end of this chapter, it's really important to know the background of the mobile world and to have thorough knowledge of former mobile technologies. Later in this chapter I describe the different mobile app types and the app business models and provide you with a short overview of the current state of mobile app stores.

Let's start with the word *mobile*. It comes from the Latin word *mobilis*, which itself is derived from the Latin verb *movere*, "to move"—to be able to move around freely and easily by walking, driving, or flying.

This definition sounds really simple and comprehensible, and I'm sure you had something similar in mind. If you look at the word *mobile* from a technological point of view, it's not quite as simple due to the vast changes in the way people have begun to use mobile technologies over the past few decades.

So let's go back a few decades in time.

Overview of Mobile Networks

Before we can communicate with any kind of mobile device, a communication infrastructure must be available. The mobile infrastructure is currently in its fourth generation, known aptly as 4G or LTE (Long-Term Evolution).[1] Before that we saw the generations 0G, 1G, 2G, and 3G, and each generation was a milestone at its time of introduction.

---

1. www.etsi.org/technologies-clusters/technologies/mobile/long-term-evolution

The zero generation—the early predecessors—included just analog radio communication and was mainly used in the 1960s. It is also known as the Mobile Radio Telephone System. Communication at this time was half duplex, meaning that only one person was able to talk at a time while the other listened. The zero generation consisted of different mobile technologies such as Mobile Telephone Service (MTS), Mobile Telephony System D (MTD), Advanced Mobile Telephone System (AMTS), and Offentlig Landmobil Telefoni (OLT). The cell phones were really heavy and were installed mostly in trucks, trains, and other vehicles. The phone consisted of two parts, the **transceiver** (transmitter and receiver) and the **head**. The transceiver was responsible for establishing the connection to the local transmitter stations, and the head was wired to the transceiver and consisted of dial keys, a display, and a handset. This generation had a lot of problems with connectivity and had limited numbers of subscribers.

The first-generation (1G) cellular network was an improvement over the zero generation and was introduced in the 1980s. 1G still used analog radio signals to transmit information using the Advanced Mobile Phone Service (AMPS) or Nordic Mobile Telephone (NMT) technology. The first networks were launched in Japan, followed by Denmark, Finland, Norway, Sweden, and the United States. A couple of years later other countries built up their 1G network infrastructure. The biggest advantage over the zero generation was that 1G was able to accommodate up to ten times more users by dividing the local area into smaller cells. This generation had its drawbacks when it came to security as users were able to listen to someone else's conversation and hack the system to make free calls.

The biggest improvement in mobile communication networks was introduced with the second generation of cellular networks. 2G was first launched in 1991 in Finland using the GSM (Global System for Mobile Communications) standard.[2] A couple of years later CDMA (Code Division Multiple Access) was launched in the United States.[3] These new standards formed the basis of today's mobile communication infrastructure and offered three main advantages over their predecessors:

- For the first time ever, communication was digital and encrypted.
- 2G was way more efficient and provided better global cell phone coverage.
- Data services were introduced, the most commonly known one being the SMS.

---

2. www.etsi.org/technologies-clusters/technologies/mobile/gsm
3. www.etsi.org/technologies-clusters/technologies/mobile/w-cdma

The 2G network was built mainly for voice and text communication and only has slow data transmission. After the 2G networks were established, mobile services usage increased and data transmission became too slow. To achieve higher data transfer rates, the 2G network was extended with the GPRS (General Packet Radio Service)[4] and EDGE (Enhanced Data rates for Global Evolution)[5] standards. GPRS is also called 2.5G and EDGE, 2.75G. Both technologies have higher data transfer rates (GPRS = 56 Kbit/s up to 115 Kbit/s, EDGE = up to 236 Kbit/s) than the normal 2G network and are the predecessors of the 3G network.

The third generation of mobile networks (3G) has been around since 2001 and is an evolution of the existing 2G networks. The third generation uses the UMTS (Universal Mobile Telecommunications System)[6] and CDMA2000 standards. 3G offers high-speed data transfer rates up to 21 Mbit/s depending on the user's current location. This high data transfer rate allows smartphone, tablet, or computer users to make video calls, watch mobile TV, and surf the Internet while on the move. The 3G networks with their high-speed data transfer rates have had a major influence on the success of mobile devices and apps.

The fourth generation of mobile communication networks accommodated the huge amounts of data now being transferred over the network by increasing data transfer rates even further. The 4G network is basically divided into two standards: WiMAX (Worldwide Interoperability for Microwave Access)[7] and LTE. WiMAX offers a download transfer rate of up to 128 Mbit/s and an upload rate of up to 56 Mbit/s. LTE offers download rates of up to 100 Mbit/s and an upload rate of up to 50Mbit/s. If both standards are fully implemented, the download speed can increase to 1 Gbit/s.

Depending on your network provider and country, your smartphone is connected to either a WiMAX or LTE network. If your phone supports 4G networks, you will see a little LTE or 4G icon in the status bar of the phone.

The fifth generation of mobile networks is currently under development. Several research groups have been formed to describe and develop the next generation of mobile communication and architecture. However, this standard will not be available before 2020.[8]

This was a high-level overview of the technology behind mobile networks, but even this high-level view is important when you start testing your app in different networks using different standards. It's important to know what kind

---

4. www.etsi.org/index.php/technologies-clusters/technologies/mobile/gprs
5. www.etsi.org/index.php/technologies-clusters/technologies/mobile/edge
6. www.etsi.org/technologies-clusters/technologies/mobile/umts
7. www.wimaxforum.org/index.htm
8. http://europa.eu/rapid/press-release_IP-13-159_en.htm

of network standards are available and which network speeds are provided. Further information on how to test the different data networks will be provided in later chapters. I highly recommend that you use this knowledge in your daily app testing.

Mobile Devices and the Year 2007

Prior to 2007 most phones were so-called feature phones (as described in Chapter 1, "What's Special about Mobile Testing?") whose functionality could not be extended with software (apps). Not all of them were able to connect to the Internet, even when the mobile networks were able to handle data transmission. At that time Nokia, Motorola, BlackBerry (Research in Motion), and some other mobile manufacturers dominated the mobile device market. Most of the devices had a small screen and a physical keyboard and were good just for making a call or typing a text message. However, those devices were no fun to use when trying to surf the Web or search for contacts within the phone.

The smartphone revolution started in January 2007 when Apple launched its first iPhone. Steve Jobs presented the first generation of the iPhone with the following sentence: "Today, Apple is going to reinvent the phone."

And Steve Jobs was right. The mobile device market has of course changed dramatically since 2007. Just one year later, Google presented the first Android smartphone developed by HTC, the HTC Dream (also known as T-Mobile G1). In the following years lots of other manufacturers built their own Android smartphones with different Android software versions.

When Apple announced the iPhone, only Google was fast enough to adapt and build another mobile platform. However, Microsoft and BlackBerry (Research in Motion) have updated their mobile technologies to close the gap between themselves and Apple and Google, but until now they still haven't managed to catch up.

Since 2007, smartphones have constantly been improved with new hardware and software features, and sometimes it's hard to follow all the new features that are rolled out into the mobile market.

You need to know what's inside a smartphone to get an overview of its physical parts and what each of them does. This knowledge will help you understand the devices you want to test, which in turn will help you test more effectively.

If you look at the mobile device next to you, you will see a small, thin, and flat or curved piece of glass, plastic, or metal. All the hardware that is needed to bring this little thing to life is packed into the small case and is not seen by the user. But what's inside?

A typical smartphone consists of the following hardware components:

- Mainboard or logic board
- CPU (central processing unit)
- GPU (graphics processing unit)
- Memory
- Different antennas and interfaces:
  - Cellular network chips to connect to 2G, 3G, or 4G
  - Wi-Fi
  - NFC (near field communication)
  - GPS (Global Positioning System)
  - Bluetooth
- Various sensors (not necessarily all of the ones in this list):
  - Ambient light sensor
  - Proximity sensor
  - Acceleration sensor
  - Gyroscope
  - Magnetic sensor
  - Pressure sensor
  - Temperature sensor
  - Humidity sensor
- Battery
- Vibration motor
- Slot for additional memory card
- Slot for SIM card

Here are the parts you can see when you have your smartphone in your hand:

- Smartphone case
- Touchscreen

- Hardware buttons (power button, volume up and down button, navigation buttons)
- Headphone jack
- Speakers and microphones
- Charger/USB connector
- Front and rear cameras
- Flash

If you want to get more detailed information about a specific phone, just use the Internet and search for "teardowns" of the device or check out the device manufacturer's Web site. The hardware I listed also applies to tablets with some variations.

As a mobile tester, it's very important that you know all the possible components within a mobile device. This knowledge is needed to identify and narrow down problems or bugs that could be related to the device hardware or your app.

The Big Two

As mentioned in the previous chapter, other mobile platforms such as Windows Phone and BlackBerry have very little market share compared to Android and iOS.[9] As of February 2015, market shares were as follows: Android, 55.26%; iOS, 23.82%; Windows Phone, 2.32%; and BlackBerry, 1.66%. The missing 17% includes devices running Symbian, Series 40, and other outdated mobile operating systems.

> **Important**   These figures will of course vary depending on geographical location, but they're a good indicator of the big picture.

Since BlackBerry and Windows Phone have very little market share, I'll focus on the big two for the rest of the chapter: iOS and Android.

What are the differences between the two operating systems? What do they have in common? Table 2.1 compares the operating systems based on certain criteria.

---

9. Exact figures on market share can be found here: http://gs.statcounter.com

Table 2.1 *Comparison of Android and iOS*

Criteria	Android	iOS
Company	Google	Apple
OS family	Linux	OS X, Linux
Programmed in	C, C++; apps in Java	C, C++; apps in Objective-C, Swift (since iOS 8)
Source model	Open source	Closed source
Open source	Kernel, UI, and some of the standard apps	iOS kernel not open source but based on open-source Darwin OS
Manufacturer	LG, Samsung, HTC, Sony, ASUS, Motorola, Huawei, . . .	Apple
Customizability	Almost everything can be changed	Very limited
Widgets	Yes, on the desktop as well as in the notification center	Yes, within the notification center
Interfaces	Touchscreen	Touchscreen
Voice commands	Google Now	Siri
Maps	Google Maps	Apple Maps
Video chat	Hangout	FaceTime
Available languages	32 languages	34 languages
App store	Google Play, Amazon, Samsung, . . .	Apple App Store

As you can see, both platforms have lots of technologies, functions, and apps in common, such as apps for voice commands, maps, video chats, e-mail, a calendar, and much more. But if you look at the source model and programming languages, you'll notice the main differences. Parts of the open-source Android operating system are written in C and C++. Android apps are written in Java. iOS is also written in C and C++ and is closed source. iOS apps are written in Objective-C or Swift. iOS uses the open-source Darwin operating system as a system basis, but the finished iOS version as we know it is closed source.

Another obvious difference between the two is the manufacturers. Apple produces iOS devices on its own, whereas Google gives other manufacturers the opportunity to build their own hardware devices based on the Android operating system. The manufacturers are able to extend the raw Android operating system and build a customized Android version tailored to the hardware.

Mobile testers need to know all about the tailoring of the different hardware manufacturers because the user interfaces on Android can differ a lot and therefore influence the behavior of an app. The fragmentation of Android devices and software versions is one of the main challenges that mobile testers need to handle. However, there is also a pure Android device available on the market as Google cooperates with some hardware manufacturers to build their Nexus devices.

Last, I want to point out the differences between the user interfaces. Both platforms provide touch interfaces that have lots of gestures in common such as swiping, tapping, pinch, and zoom, but each has its own UI and design patterns. For complete instructions check the Android design guide[10] and the iOS design guide.[11] With each new version of the operating system, check those guidelines again, because changes are likely. These patterns must be followed in order to publish an app. If your app doesn't follow the guidelines, it may well be rejected from the app store, which is more likely to happen in the Apple App Store than in the Android app stores. To get an overview of possible reasons why an app is rejected from an app store, look at the "Common App Rejections" page provided by Apple.[12]

Another good reason to follow the design principles is to make customers happy because they know how to use the platform-specific features such as swiping from left to right to switch views, or to pull down to refresh the current view.

When the device has booted, both platforms present a home screen to the user that is similar to a computer desktop. While the iOS home screen contains only rows of app icons spread over several home screens, Android gives the user the ability to customize the home screen with apps and widgets.[13] Widgets are able to display more information on the desktop, such as content from the e-mail app, Twitter, or the weather. Widgets can be resized and placed wherever the user wants to have them. Since iOS 8, users are able to place widgets in the iOS notification center as well.

Both home screens have a dock section at the bottom of the screen to pin the most important apps that are available on every home screen. Also, both platforms have a status bar that is available at the top of the screen and displays device-relevant information such as the battery status, the network strength, the current time, and any notifications from installed apps. Again, on Android

10. https://developer.android.com/design/index.html
11. https://developer.apple.com/design/
12. https://developer.apple.com/app-store/review/rejections/
13. https://developer.android.com/guide/topics/appwidgets/index.html

the status bar can display more information such as received e-mails, messages, phone calls, or reminders linked to installed apps.

If you're familiar with only one platform, you should buy or rent the unfamiliar one to learn everything about it. You will need to know as much as possible about the major platforms to succeed in the long run as a mobile tester.

What Types of Apps Exist?

If you unlock your phone to get to the home screen, you will see your installed apps. But which types of apps do you have installed? Are they native, hybrid, or Web-based applications? If you just look at the app icon, you probably can't tell. Maybe you can find out by tapping on an app icon to open it.

Let's try it out. Get your mobile device, unlock it, and open an app of your choice.

What do you see? Is a browser window shown, or is the app visible in full-screen mode? If you see a browser window, your app is a Web-based application.

But can you see the difference between a hybrid and a native app? That will depend on how well the hybrid app is developed and optimized for your phone.

In the following section I will describe the different mobile app types and list the pros and cons of each of them.

Native Apps

Native apps are programmed with a specific programming language for the specific mobile platform. For example, Android apps are developed in Java, whereas iOS apps are written in Objective-C or Swift. Native apps have full access to all platform-specific libraries and APIs in order to take advantage of all the features a modern smartphone has to offer. Assuming the user has granted the necessary permissions, the app has direct access to the camera, GPS, and all the other sensors. Developers are able to build apps that make use of system resources such as the GPU and CPU to build powerful apps. Native apps generally exhibit excellent performance and are optimized for mobile platforms. In most cases, native apps look and feel great and are able to support every possible gesture on the touchscreen.

App distribution is also quite simple as you can upload your native app to the app stores of the different vendors and start selling it. Some app store vendors have an approval process, meaning that it can take some time until your app is available. The same process applies when an already released app is updated, which can be a problem especially when you want to fix a really urgent bug in your app.

Pros:

- Native apps have full access to platform-specific hardware and software features.

- Native apps have good performance because they are optimized for the specific mobile platform.

- Native apps have a good look-and-feel.

- Native apps offer good usability if the platform UI guidelines are met.

- Native apps have full access to all touch gestures (if implemented).

- Native app distribution is easy. Users can search for your app.

- Native apps can store data offline.

Cons:

- The amount of development work increases with each supported platform because each platform needs its own code base.

- The approval process can be quite long.

- Updating a released app may take some time (which is annoying when it comes to urgent bug fixes).

- Development costs can be higher.

- You must share 30% of your app revenues with the platform provider.

Hybrid Apps

Hybrid apps, as the name suggests, are apps that consist of different Web technologies such as HTML or JavaScript. Once the Web part has been built, developers are able to compile this code base to the different native formats: Android, iOS, Windows Phone, or BlackBerry. To compile the Web code into native mobile code, developers need to use a hybrid development framework such as PhoneGap.[14] Such frameworks offer APIs to access the device-specific hardware features within the Web part of the app.

How does such a framework work?

> **Important** The description here is a very simplistic view of hybrid mobile frameworks.

---

14. http://phonegap.com/

The framework builds a so-called bridge to the Web code via an HTML rendering engine. A small part of the app runs on the native operating system and communicates with the Web code in the rendering engine via the bridge. With the aid of this bridge, the Web code can access some of the native hardware features.

The HTML content or components of hybrid apps can be hosted on a server. This approach makes it very easy to make small updates without updating the whole app through the app store submission process. Storing the information and elements on the server has one big drawback; however, the content and elements don't work when the phone is offline. These parts are available only if the device is connected to a data network. However, you can put all the content and elements into the app for full offline support, but then small online updates are no longer possible. If your team is developing a hybrid app, keep those points in mind.

Pros:

- There is one code base for different mobile platforms.
- Frameworks offer access to hardware features.
- Small updates can be performed on the server.
- App distribution is easy.
- Users can search for your app.

Cons:

- Performance is bad when the content and components are accessed from the server.
- Meeting the design guidelines of the different mobile platforms is not easy.
- Platform-specific features can't be developed, because they may not be available on the other platforms.
- The approval process may be long.

A nice comparison of different mobile development frameworks can be found on the "Mobile Frameworks Comparison Chart" Web site.[15]

---

15. http://mobile-frameworks-comparison-chart.com/

Web Apps

A mobile Web app is a Web site that can be accessed from the device's Web browser. Such Web sites are optimized for mobile browser usage and are independent of the mobile platform. Mobile Web apps are developed with Web technologies such as HTML and JavaScript, particularly with HTML5,[16] CSS3, and JavaScript.[17]

HTML5 offers developers the capability to implement mobile Web sites with animated and interactive elements. They can integrate audio or video files and use positioning features as well as some local storage functionality. The use of HTML5, CSS3, and JavaScript makes it easy to develop mobile Web apps. Furthermore, mobile Web apps require no app store approval and can be easily and quickly updated.

However, mobile Web apps have some drawbacks. For example, they offer only very limited to no access to the device hardware features such as proximity or acceleration sensors. Mobile Web apps have no access to the camera, compass, microphone, or any kind of notifications. They tend to be slower than native or hybrid apps because they need to download all the information that is shown on the screen.

Depending on the mobile browser, mobile Web apps can work and behave differently because not all mobile browsers support the full standards of HTML5, CSS3, and JavaScript. This can have a major influence on the mobile Web app, meaning that different mobile Web browsers need to be covered during the testing process.

To summarize, Web apps have the following advantages and disadvantages:

Pros:

- Popular technologies are used for development.
- Web apps are faster and cheaper to implement than native and hybrid apps.
- They are mobile platform independent.
- There is easy access to them via a Web browser (no installation required).
- No app store submission is required.
- The updating process is fast and easy.

16. http://dev.w3.org/html5/html-author/
17. www.w3.org/Style/CSS/

Cons:

- There is limited access to hardware features.

- There is limited offline behavior.

- Large media files such as images or videos can take a long time to download.

- They have different Web browser support for the HTML5, CSS3, and JavaScript standards.

- They are not as convenient to use as native apps.

- There is limited usage of touch gestures.

- Users can't find the app in the app stores.

Business Models of Mobile Apps

Where's the money in mobile apps? And how can you test to make sure money is being earned? These two questions are important when developing and testing an app. Nearly every app developer and company wants to make money from in-app purchases!

You therefore need to test the payment models to be sure that the mobile app is generating revenues, which in turn means that you need to be aware of current business models:

- Freemium
- Paid
- Transaction

Freemium

The freemium model is designed to reach as many users as possible.

Once the app is installed, there are several ways to generate revenues out of the free app:

- The most widely used approach is the free version of the app. The free version is limited, such as in terms of functionality or content. If a user wants to have full functionality, he or she can download the enhanced (paid) version of the app. This approach is the most widely used freemium app model.

- The second most used approach for generating revenues is selling advertisements within the app. There are different kinds of advertisement formats that can be added to an app in order to generate revenues. Advertisements are part of nearly every free app and can often be really annoying and frustrating for the user. Think very carefully before adding ads to an app as you run the risk of losing customers. Developers can implement ad frameworks such as AdMob[18] or iAd.[19]

- The third approach for generating revenues is the "in-app purchase." This is often used within gaming apps where new levels or more tools can be bought to have more fun with the game. Lots of newspaper apps also offer in-app purchases to get the latest version of their daily news. Some apps can become ad free if the user pays for it.

Paid

The paid business model is quite simple: before users can download the app, they have to pay for it. This is a common use case for gaming apps or apps that fulfill a special task such as applying filters to images to make them look like Polaroids.

Transaction

In the transaction business model the user pays only after completing a transaction with the app. An example of a transactional app is Google Wallet, where users are able to send money to another account using their credit or debit card.[20] Once the transaction is complete, a small fee is paid that depends on the transaction amount.

Choosing a Business Model

Research carried out by Gartner shows that freemium apps containing in-app purchases are downloaded the most (approximately 90%) from the app stores, whereas paid apps are downloaded far less frequently.[21] Developers therefore need to put some thought into their app's business model and price.

When choosing a business model for your app, make sure you keep the different app types in mind. Not every model can be applied to every app type. For

---

18. www.google.com/ads/admob/
19. http://advertising.apple.com/
20. www.google.com/wallet/
21. www.gartner.com/newsroom/id/2592315

example, if you want to develop a paid mobile Web app, your app needs a login to identify the user's subscription so as to gain access to the paid content. The login function may not be necessary within a native or hybrid app because payment is made within the app store.

App Stores

App stores form the core of the mobile world where apps can be downloaded and reviewed. Without the app stores, smartphones wouldn't be as intelligent and functional as we want them to be. At the time of writing, the app stores of the biggest mobile platforms—Google[22] and Apple[23]—contain more than two million apps. So far more than 100 billion app downloads have been counted. These are huge numbers that are bound to increase in the future.

Besides the big two app stores from Apple and Google, there are other stores sponsored by device manufacturers and network operators. The following list is not complete but contains some other app stores for the different mobile platforms:

- Amazon
- AT&T
- China Mobile
- Mozilla
- Samsung
- T-Mobile
- Vodafone

But why are there so many different stores? Especially in the Android world there is more than one app store available, such as the Amazon[24] and Samsung[25] stores. The answer to this question is simple: every app store provider wants to make money out of the mobile app business!

Let's take the Samsung store as an example. Since the launch of its Galaxy device series, Samsung has grown to become one of the biggest and most successful Android device manufacturers and has sold and continues to sell millions of devices around the world. Having its own app store preinstalled on

---

22. Google Play store, https://play.google.com/store
23. Apple App Store, https://itunes.apple.com/us/genre/ios/id36?mt=8
24. www.amazon.com/mobile-apps/b?node=2350149011
25. http://apps.samsung.com/

every Samsung phone is a huge advantage because it directs potential mobile app customers straight to Samsung and away from Google. If millions of users use this store, the store generates traffic, which means it can sell ads. On top of that, app sales via the app store allow Samsung to generate additional revenues. In most of the app stores, 30% of the sale price goes to the platform provider, and the same applies to in-app purchases.

I think this is indicative of why there are so many different mobile app stores. If you search the Internet, I'm sure you'll find even more of them.

The other mobile platforms also have app stores. BlackBerry apps can be downloaded from the official BlackBerry World,[26] and Windows Phone apps can be downloaded from the Microsoft Store.[27]

Before a mobile team distributes an app in the biggest stores, they should think about the goals of the app. Maybe there are other stores that are better suited to their app than the big players. For example, some stores offer a better revenue share than the usual 70% (developer revenues)/30% (store provider revenues) split, or they offer better app targeting, for example, in different markets such as Africa or Asia.

However, uploading an app to one of the stores requires one thing in particular—knowledge of the store's review and publishing process. Your app needs to fulfill the review and publishing guidelines of the various vendors and app stores; otherwise your app is very likely to be rejected.

Knowledge of the different review guidelines will allow you to better support your team while developing and releasing your app. The review and publishing guidelines of the major mobile app stores can be found on the following Web sites:

- Amazon Appstore Guidelines (https://developer.amazon.com/help/faq .html)
- Apple App Store Guidelines (https://developer.apple.com/app-store/ review/)
- BlackBerry World Guidelines (http://developer.blackberry.com/blackberry world/vp_checklist.html)
- Google Play store Guidelines (http://developer.android.com/distribute/ googleplay/publish/preparing.html)

---

26. BlackBerry World, http://appworld.blackberry.com/webstore/?d=android&o=m&countrycode =US&lang=en
27. Microsoft Store, www.windowsphone.com/en-us/store

- Samsung App Store Guidelines (http://developer.samsung.com/distribute/app-submission-guide)
- Windows Phone Store Guidelines (http://msdn.microsoft.com/en-us/library/windows/apps/br230835.aspx)

Summary

Chapter 2 covered the evolution of mobile data networks and mobile devices. It is very important to know the differences among the data networks, their speed, and their technologies. This knowledge is required when testing a mobile app while you are on the move.

Besides the data networks, knowledge about mobile devices and their evolution is also very important. A mobile tester must know all the hardware and software components of a modern smartphone in order to test mobile apps in various situations and with different hardware and software combinations.

In a later section of this chapter I explained the different app types that are currently available on the market. The differences among a native, hybrid, and Web app as well as their pros and cons should be clear by now.

The different business models for mobile apps were explained. The closing section of this chapter dealt with the different mobile app stores that are available for each platform and what is important to know about them.

Chapter 3

Challenges in Mobile Testing

In Chapter 1, "What's Special about Mobile Testing?" I described the unique aspects of mobile testing, covering user expectations, data networks, mobile devices, and mobile release cycles. But there are, of course, other topics that make mobile testing a special and challenging job.

This chapter contains more mobile testing challenges together with their possible solutions.

The Customer

As I mentioned in Chapter 1, customers and their expectations are one of the main challenges for mobile developers and testers.

To satisfy customers, it's really important that you gather information about your possible target customers and their needs. If you release an app without any kind of knowledge of your target group, the app will most likely not be installed or it will receive really bad reviews. This leads to fewer downloads, and customers may even download an app from your competitor.

In order to handle the customer challenge, you need to gather as much information about your potential users as possible. This, in turn, means that you need to incorporate the specifics of your target group, such as age, gender, and geographical background, during the development and testing process. You need information such as the following:

- Gender
- Age

- Monthly income (important for possible app business models)
- Educational background
- Geographical background (e.g., do they live in a city?)
- What apps they use and what kind
- Smartphone habits (how often they check their smartphone)
- Whether they use a competitor's apps and if so, how, and are they happy with them
- What devices they use

Important   Be careful when asking people personal questions as you could end up infringing upon privacy laws.

Another way of getting information about your target group is to conduct interviews: invite your customers to your office and ask them about their mobile usage and habits. If you encounter problems getting the answers to all of these questions or are not allowed to ask your potential customers directly, you can use services such as Mobile Personas[1] to get general information about the behavior of mobile users.

If you gather, analyze, and group that kind of information, you will most likely have more than one type of person the app will be made for. To satisfy the different types of customers, it is helpful to create so-called personas[2] to represent their various needs. Personas were introduced by Alan Cooper[3] in 1998 in his book *The Inmates Are Running the Asylum*.

Personas are fictional characters that are representative of your real customers. Personas are a common and very useful way to identify user motivations, expectations, problems, habits, and goals.

Personas can help you to make decisions about your app, such as feature set, possible gestures, and design. Personas can help a mobile team get a feel for their customers' needs and problems. You as a mobile tester can align your daily workflow to the persona description. Table 3.1 presents an example of a typical persona.

---

1. www.mobilepersonas.com/
2. www.usability.gov/how-to-and-tools/methods/personas.html
3. www.cooper.com/journal/2008/05/the_origin_of_personas

Table 3.1 *Possible Persona Description*

Information	Profile
Name	Martin
Gender	Male
Age	28
Monthly income	$3,000
Educational background	Master's degree in computer science
Location	Greater New York area
Uses the following apps	Twitter, Facebook, LinkedIn, Feedly, Spotify, Tumblr
Checks his smartphone . . . times a day	150
Devices owned	LG Google Nexus 5, iPad mini
Personal traits	Friendly, smart, polite, likes to meet friends

You can also write a persona description, such as this one:

Martin is a 28-year-old tech-savvy male with a master's degree in computer science. He lives in New York and is a frequent smartphone user who checks his smartphone around 150 times a day. Martin uses apps like Twitter, Facebook, Spotify, and Tumblr. His monthly income is about $3,000. Martin is a friendly, smart, and polite person who likes to meet friends.

With the aid of personas and knowledge of their habits, it's a bit easier to test a mobile app as the testing process is more focused on customer needs than on the tester's expectations or habits.

Personas are a good way to handle the customer challenge when it comes to mobile testing. Once the personas are in place, the mobile team should try to find real customers who match the personas. Once you've found some customers, talk to them and ask them questions about your app and discuss possible additional features. Invite users to a usability testing session in your office. This way the users feel connected with the company and your app. Another way of getting user feedback or engagement is a beta testing phase. This is a common approach; some big mobile app vendors[4] invite customers to test beta

---

4. www.sonos.com/beta/screen/

versions of new apps to collect feedback at an early development stage so they can improve the app before going live.

Other valuable sources of information about your customers are the app stores of the different vendors and the ratings for and comments about your app. Read the comments carefully and learn from them. Of course, there may be lots of comments that don't deliver any useful insights. However, there are users who complain about usability, bugs, or problems you have never heard of, and those comments are extremely useful for you and your team. More information about app store reviews, ratings, and comments can be found in Chapter 7, "Mobile Test and Launch Strategies."

Customer Summary

Do the following in order to maximize the chances that you will satisfy your customers:

- Gather user information.
- Create personas.
- Use personas while testing.
- Invite customers to usability tests.
- Interview customers about your product.
- Invite customers to be beta testers.
- Check the app store reviews and learn from the useful comments.

Mobile Platforms and Fragmentation

In the previous chapters I explained the different mobile vendors and mobile platforms, so you now know what's inside a mobile device. You also know that for some mobile platforms there is more than one mobile device manufacturer.

Fragmentation is a huge problem in the mobile world and especially in the Android world. Based on the numbers from OpenSignal,[5] nearly 19,000 Android devices are available on the market. It's simply not possible and, as you will see, not necessary to test on all of those devices. This problem isn't just limited to Android; other mobile platforms such as iOS, Windows Phone, and BlackBerry are also affected by fragmentation. The possible hardware and software combinations on those platforms can also be a problem.

---

5. http://opensignal.com/reports/2014/android-fragmentation/

The next several sections of this chapter present some solutions for handling fragmentation while testing.

Mobile Device Groups

One solution for handling device fragmentation in your mobile testing project is to group your mobile test devices. If the devices are grouped, you can test on only some devices (one to three) from each group, which helps you downsize the amount of testing work. I've adopted this approach in all of my mobile projects and it has proven very efficient. Based on your target customer group, you can create three device groups (this example assumes that the target group is really tech savvy).

The first group has the highest priority: A. Devices in this group are most likely to be new devices with powerful hardware and a big screen with a high resolution and pixel density. They also usually have the latest operating system version installed. Devices in this group must be fully supported by your app in terms of functionality, design, and usability.

- **Group 1, Priority A:**
  - High-end devices
  - Dual/quad-core CPU
  - RAM >=2,048MB
  - Display size >=5"
  - Retina, full HD display
  - Latest operating system that is available for the device

The second group has medium priority: B. Devices in this group are mid-range devices with average hardware such as a smaller CPU, screen resolution, and size than the devices in group A. The operating system version is probably less than one year old. The devices in this group should fully support the app in terms of functionality and usability. The design doesn't need to be perfect for this group due to the smaller screens.

- **Group 2, Priority B:**
  - Midrange devices
  - Dual-core CPU
  - RAM <2,048MB
  - Display size <5"

- No Retina or full HD display
- Software less than one year old

The third group has low priority: C. Devices in this group have a small CPU and a small screen resolution and density. The software version is more than one year old. Devices in this group still have to fully support the app in terms of functionality, but the design and usability may differ from the other groups because the hardware may be too slow to provide sufficient responsiveness.

- **Group 3, Priority C:**
  - Slow devices
  - Single-core CPU
  - RAM <1,024MB
  - Display size <4″
  - Low screen resolution
  - Operating system more than one year old

Once you have defined device groups, you need to make sure you keep them current by monitoring the mobile device market for new devices that match your target groups. On the other hand, you can remove older devices from your device groups if your customers don't use them anymore. And last but not least, you need to check your group criteria from time to time to make sure they still sufficiently cover your customer spectrum.

With the aid of such device groups, you'll find it much easier to handle device fragmentation and have the right devices for testing.

A nice Web page provided by Google is "Our Mobile Planet,"[6] where you can get information based on the country, the age, the gender, and the behavior of users. Such information can be used when the target customer is unknown.

> **Important**   Device groups may vary greatly from project to project!

Mobile Device Labs

Depending on the mobile app project, you may need lots of devices for testing, which is of course very expensive and time-consuming. A good alternative to buying all of your testing devices is to rent them.

---

6. http://think.withgoogle.com/mobileplanet/en/

You can use mobile device labs or device clouds to rent the testing devices you need. However, before you rent test devices, keep the device grouping in mind to downsize the amount of testing required for all those virtual and physical devices.

Currently there are plenty of mobile device lab providers that offer mobile test devices within the cloud. Mobile developers and testers are able to upload the app file to the cloud, select the devices, and start manual or automated testing.

The main advantage of such services is that you don't have to worry about buying new devices and maintaining them. However, before choosing a mobile cloud provider, you should check whether the provider offers testing on real devices, simulators, or emulators.

A mobile cloud testing provider should:

- Test on real devices
- Be able to use emulators or simulators as well
- Not use jailbroken or rooted devices
- Be able to test on different mobile platforms if possible
- Be able to write test automation scripts in different programming languages
- Offer continuous integration
- Have some performance monitoring in place
- Generate a test report at the end of the test cycle

Testing your mobile app in the cloud on emulators or simulators can be very annoying due to performance issues. Using emulators or simulators on a local machine is often already fairly slow; using them on the Internet via a Web GUI can be even slower.

Even if the provider offers testing on real devices, it's still possible that the performance may not be the same as when testing on a local physical device. The latency may be too high, which can lead to very slow reactions on the device. Scrolling, tapping, or just loading the app can take a long time, which may have a big impact on your testing and the subsequent results.

Another thing to look out for when choosing a cloud provider is to make sure you have exclusive access to the physical devices and that your app is deleted once the test session is complete. Check that the provider offers a private test cloud; otherwise your app may still be installed on the test devices for subsequent customers to see. Discovering such an issue while evaluating a provider is a clear warning sign that should not be ignored. If security and privacy are important to you, consider picking another provider.

The following providers offer a mobile device test cloud:

- AppThwack (https://appthwack.com/)
- CloudMonkey LabManager (www.cloudmonkeymobile.com/labmanager)
- Keynote Mobile Testing (www.keynotedeviceanywhere.com/)
- Mobile Labs (http://mobilelabsinc.com/)
- Perfecto Mobile (www.perfectomobile.com/)
- Sauce Labs (https://saucelabs.com/)
- Testmunk (www.testmunk.com/)
- TestObject (http://testobject.com/)
- TouchTest (www.soasta.com/products/touchtest/)
- Xamarin Test Cloud (http://xamarin.com/test-cloud)

Important   This list is by no means complete. Just browse the Internet to search for more providers that fit in your environment.

If you don't want to buy every testing device for your company or don't want to use a cloud provider (or maybe you're not allowed to use one), there is another way of getting physical mobile devices: ODLs, or Open Device Labs.

Open Device Labs were introduced by the mobile community with the aim of establishing physical stores where mobile testers, developers, and anyone involved in the mobile business can obtain devices for testing purposes. The primary goal of these Open Device Labs is that everyone can borrow devices for free! In order to make this idea successful, Open Device Labs need device donations from individuals or companies who want to support the mobile community. Depending on your geographical region, you might have an Open Device Lab nearby. The Web site[7] provides a nice map that shows you where your nearest Open Device Lab is located. You should definitely try them!

Chapter 7 includes mobile test labs and Open Device Labs as part of the mobile testing strategy and also provides further information on this topic.

In this part of the chapter you have learned that there are three possible solutions to the problem of how to handle mobile fragmentation:

- Grouping the devices you need for testing
- Mobile device labs in the cloud
- Using physical devices from an Open Device Lab

---

7. http://opendevicelab.com/

Sensors and Interfaces

Every smartphone has a variety of sensors and interfaces that can be accessed by the installed apps to provide useful features to users. The actual sensors and interfaces used depend on the app's specific use case. The installed sensors and interfaces are really complex and are potentially susceptible to electrical interference.

As a mobile tester it's your responsibility to ensure that the implemented sensors and interfaces are used correctly. It's also important to verify that failing sensors don't affect the app in a negative way.

Ambient Light Sensor

The ambient light sensor is able to determine how much light is available in the current location and automatically adjust the screen's brightness by means of software in order to prolong the device's battery life.

If your app makes use of the ambient light sensor in any way, you should test your app in different locations with different prevailing light situations. For example, test your app in a dark room, outside in the sunshine, or at your workplace to see if the app responds correctly. Be creative with your testing environments.

Different locations could include:

- A dark room
- Your workplace with a desk lamp on
- Outside in the sunshine
- Rooms with different lights on the ceiling

Proximity Sensor

Another little helper is the proximity sensor, which determines how close the phone is located, such as to a face or surface. It can be used to automatically turn off the display without any physical contact. This prevents you from accidentally clicking or touching buttons on an active screen. It's also useful for saving battery life.

Make sure you also test the usage of the proximity sensor in different locations with different light situations as well as with different kinds of surfaces to see whether the app is using the sensor correctly.

Different locations and surfaces could include the following:

- A dark room
- Your workplace with a desk lamp on
- Outside in the sunshine
- Your hand moving over the display
- Your hand close to the display
- The device moving toward your face
- The device's display moving toward a mirror or pane of glass

Acceleration Sensor

The acceleration sensor detects changes in the device's movement. The most common use case for this sensor is when the device is rotated between portrait and landscape modes. This sensor is used in nearly every app if the developers implemented a portrait and landscape view. If both modes are supported, you should change the orientation of the device a lot during testing. By doing so, you will probably find lots of UI glitches because the UI elements could be moved to a different position. It is also likely that the app will crash, for example, when data is fetched from the backend while a UI refresh is being performed.

Gyroscope Sensor

The gyroscope sensor is used to either measure or maintain the orientation of the device. Unlike an accelerometer, which measures the linear acceleration of a device, a gyroscope measures the device's exact orientation. This means that the device is able to detect 360-degree motion. Thanks to the accelerometer and gyroscope sensors, the device is able to operate on six axes—left and right, up and down, forward and backward—and track roll, yaw, and pitch rotations.

The combination of both sensors is mostly used in gaming apps such as flight simulations to control a plane with real physical movements. Keep the six axes in mind when testing your app, and test each axis separately as well as multiple axes at once to be sure the app is responding correctly.

Magnetic Sensor

A magnetic sensor is able to measure the strength and orientation of magnetic fields around the device. This sensor is mostly used by apps that require compass information, such as for navigation. With the aid of this sensor the device is able to determine the direction in which it's facing: west, east, north, or south.

If your app uses the magnetic sensor, you should also test it in different locations. For example, if you're using the app in a building where you're surrounded by lots of metal, the magnetic sensor may deliver false information or data, which can lead to adverse side effects in your app.

Different locations could include the following:

- Inside a building
- Outside on the street
- When stuck in traffic
- Near buildings with lots of metal

Pressure, Temperature, and Humidity Sensors

These three sensors are not included in every smartphone yet, but they will be soon. All three sensors can be used to collect more data about the user's current location to provide apps with useful information such as the current temperature, current altitude based on atmospheric pressure, and humidity.

These sensors are used, for example, by outdoor or weather apps. Again, make sure you test these sensors in different locations with different temperatures, pressures, altitudes, and humidities. You can, of course, simulate pressure or humidity in a test lab situation to check that the sensors are working correctly, but testing them in real situations could produce side effects that aren't likely to happen in a lab.

Location Sensor

You certainly know the location sensor, better known as GPS. Thanks to GPS, apps can determine the current device location. GPS is used in lots of different kinds of apps such as map apps, camera apps, and social media apps. Users can share their current location with apps and send their current position, for example, to friends to let them know where they are.

If your app uses GPS to determine the device's current position, be sure that the GPS sensor is switched off after use. Otherwise the device's battery will be empty very soon.

GPS functionality should of course be tested in various locations, such as in the countryside or in downtown sprawl with lots of huge buildings. In both scenarios you may find that the current location is incorrect or not found by

the GPS sensor. This is especially true in cities due to interference caused by sur-
rounding buildings. If the GPS signal is not strong enough to determine the current location, check that the Wi-Fi or network-based location finding feature
of the phone is activated to locate the phone. A low GPS signal can also cause
performance problems within your app due to difficulties in calculating the current position. When testing the GPS function of your app, keep an eye on the
temperature of your device. Using GPS will heat up your device, consume lots
of battery, and therefore possibly influence the performance of your app. I also
recommend that you turn GPS off to see how your app reacts to this scenario.

Touchless Sensor

Another sensor that is not built into every smartphone is a touchless sensor. In
most cases this sensor is built into the front of the device to accept touchless
gestures from a finger or a hand. What this means is that you can swipe between
photos in your photo gallery simply by waving your hand over the screen. Or
you can answer a phone call by holding the device next to your ear without
touching the answer button.

   If your app supports touchless gestures, be sure every gesture also works at
different angles.

Sensors Summary

Most of the sensors just described are influenced by the user's current location
and surroundings. Any kind of movement is very important while testing your
app and the device's sensors. It's also useful to test the sensors in combination
with one another to check that your app responds correctly to changes of sensor data.

   Possible sensor tests could include the following:

- Walk while using the app as this simulates back-and-forth motion.
- While walking, suddenly stop for a few moments before continuing on
  your way.
- Shake and rotate the device.
- Simulate vibrations as if you're on a train or in a car.
- Perform extreme movements such as spinning or rotating the device.
- Use the app outdoors in sunny, cloudy, and dark locations.
- Use the app indoors with normal light or under a lamp.
- Wave your hands in front of the device.

- Test the edge cases, for example: GPS coordinates 0,0; temperature at 0 degrees; waterproof devices in areas with high humidity.

- Check to see if the app can be used on devices that don't have built-in sensors and interfaces.

While performing these tasks, watch out for app crashes or freezes. Check that the UI elements are visible and displayed correctly on the screen, especially in different light situations. Keep an eye on the performance of the app and the smartphone's battery lifetime as well.

Touchscreen

The biggest and most important interface in smartphones is the touchscreen. Thanks to the touch-sensitive screen, users can use one or more fingers on the device to create gestures that the phone is able to convert into commands.

> **Important**   The description of touchscreen technologies here is simplified. If you want to get more detailed information about them, please do some online research.

There are basically two kinds of touchscreen technologies available. The first is the resistive screen that is made out of various layers and reacts to pressure. Usually this kind of touchscreen is made for use with a stylus. Whenever you have to sign for a parcel delivery, you probably sign on a resistive screen. This technology has one big drawback: it doesn't support multitouch gestures.

That is the reason why the second technology, capacitive touchscreens, is used in smartphones. Capacitive screens react to touch rather than pressure and support multitouch gestures.

Capacitive screens consist of an insulator, which in most cases is glass coated with a transparent conductor like indium tin oxide. Since the human body is also an electrical conductor, touching the capacitive screen results in a distortion of the screen's electrostatic field. This distortion is then converted into data that the device hardware is able to understand.

The following gestures are possible on a capacitive touchscreen:

- **Touch:** Touch the screen with a fingertip.
- **Long touch:** Touch the screen for a longer time.
- **Swipe:** Move your fingertip over the screen.
- **Tap:** Briefly touch the screen with a finger.

- **Double tap:** Briefly touch the screen with a fingertip twice.
- **Drag:** Move a finger over the screen without losing contact with the screen.
- **Multitouch:** Use two or more fingers on the screen at the same time.
- **Pinch open:** Touch the screen with two fingers and move them apart.
- **Pinch close:** Touch the screen with two fingers and bring them closer together.
- **Rotate:** Use two fingers on the screen and rotate them. Some apps, such as map apps, will rotate the content in the app.

The variety of possible touch gestures poses a special challenge while testing a mobile app. You should keep all the possible touch gestures in mind and use them while testing. A good way to see if an app can stand up to touch gestures is to use multiple fingers on the touchscreen at the same time. You should also perform several different touch gestures very quickly on the screen to see how the app reacts and handles the inputs. Also watch out for performance issues or UI glitches that can happen while using multitouch gestures.

One important factor to note about touchscreens is the current weather conditions. They can affect your fingers and prevent touches from being registered properly. Therefore, it's a good idea to also use the different gestures in different weather conditions such as on cold or hot days or on a day with high or low humidity to see how the app reacts to your gestures on the touchscreen.

Microphones

Another way of communicating with your app is by using your voice or sound. Most smartphones have more than one microphone installed. Usually there are up to three microphones, one at the front, one at the back (near the camera), and one at the bottom of the device. The three microphones ensure very good voice recording from all possible angles and regardless of the phone's position.

When testing sound inputs via the microphone, make sure you do the following:

- Test voice input indoors with normal sound and in noisy situations.
- Test the app indoors with more background noise such as in an office or restaurant.
- Test the app outdoors with background noises coming from a street or cars.

- Check that the app can handle the user muting and unmuting the phone or the microphone.

- Start other apps that generate sounds, such as music apps, and check the behavior of your app.

- Use the volume up and down buttons to increase or decrease the sound level and check the behavior of the app.

- Check that voice inputs are processed correctly.

- If the voice input is stored on the phone, check that playback is working properly.

- Test the voice input in a real-life environment (the purpose of the app).

While testing the sound inputs in all the different surroundings, watch out for input delays or distortion in the recording or playback mode. Keep an eye on the performance of the app and the phone to see if the device freezes or crashes due to a lack of hardware resources (especially when saving the inputs). And don't forget to check the digital rights management (DRM) when working with voice or sound inputs.

Camera

A typical smartphone has at least one camera, usually located at the back of the smartphone. However, most of today's smartphones already have two cameras: a rear-facing and a front-facing camera. The rear camera is used to take high-resolution pictures, and the front camera is mostly used for video chatting with a lower resolution. Also, most of the rear-facing cameras have a flash included.

Cameras are used in a variety of mobile apps for taking pictures or videos. Some apps use the camera as a scanner to capture information using OCR (optical character recognition) or other kinds of shapes. Good examples of this include QR (Quick Response) codes, scanning apps, or apps that scan business cards to transform them into digital contacts in your phone. Some apps just use the LED flash to act as a flashlight.

If your app uses the camera, test it with a variety of mobile devices that match your target customer group. Every smartphone has a unique camera with a unique lens, flash, and resolution. The different resolutions of the camera have an impact on the image size. The higher the resolution, the bigger the pictures are. Be sure to test the camera function with different resolutions and camera types in order to see if the app is able to process both small and large images.

Besides that, you should check the performance of the app while the camera mode is activated. The camera takes up a lot of the device's hardware resources, which can have an adverse impact on the app and cause it to crash or freeze. Heavy camera use can heat up the camera sensor and can cause hardware damage, so be sure that this is not possible within your app. Finally, don't forget to test that the app can use an image stabilizer to prevent the camera from taking blurry pictures. The same applies to video capturing within your app.

System Apps

Most preinstalled apps from device manufacturers are system apps. There are often preinstalled apps such as a contact app, a phone app, a calendar app, and the like. However, on most of the mobile platforms users are able to install apps that replace the system apps. The main reasons users do this is bad usability or the lack of functionality on the part of the system apps. If you check the app stores of the different vendors for calendar apps, for instance, you'll find plenty of apps with far more features than the preinstalled ones.

A really interesting example of this is keyboard apps on smartphones. Such apps are likely to have an impact on your app. On Android phones and tablets (and, since iOS 8, also on iOS devices), users are able to replace the preinstalled keyboard app with special keyboards that offer a totally different way of typing and keyboard layouts. There are conventional tap keyboards (like QWERTY), keyboards with different layouts (multiple symbols per key), keyboards with tap-slider functions, and keyboards that offer a swiping method to insert text.

Changing the keyboard can have an influence on your app. For example, the keyboard may be much taller than the standard one and therefore hide UI elements that are important to interact with, or the screen might not recognize that it needs to scroll. You may come across important keys that are missing from the keyboard, thus possibly rendering your app unusable in some cases. It is also possible for settings to get lost within your phone, and your app might cause freezes or crashes.

This is just one example of how replaced system apps can have an impact on your app. If your app interacts with one of the preinstalled system apps, keep in mind that users are able to replace them with other apps. You need to have an overview of popular apps that replace system apps in order to test their integration and interaction with your app.

Internationalization (I18n) and Localization (L10n)

Another challenge that needs to be handled during the mobile development process is the internationalization (I18n) and localization (L10n) of mobile apps. I18n is the process of designing software applications in such a way that they can be adapted to various languages and geographical regions throughout the world, without changing the code base and while the software is running (some apps and some mobile platforms require a restart).

L10n is the process of adapting the internationalized software to a specific language or region by adding locale-specific elements or translating the text.

It's really important to test both I18n and L10n if your app is designed to be used in different countries. You must be sure that the different languages will not break your UI elements or have an influence on the app's usability.

> **Important** Many languages have their own character set, and one word can have a very different width and height.

Have a look at the example word *logout*. If you compare the word with translations from Germany, France, Turkey, and Russia, you will see lots of difference in characters, width, and height:

- Logout (English)
- Ausloggen (German)
- Déconnexion (French)
- Çıkış yap (Turkish)
- Выйти (Russian)

Both the German word *Ausloggen* and the French word *Déconnexion* are much longer than *Logout*. The Turkish version even consists of two words. As a sample, Asian languages can be used as "short" languages, while German and Portuguese are considered "long" languages. All translations can lead to a UI glitch or even break your design rules. When testing an app in different languages, check that every text translation will fit into the UI elements and that every screen has the same look-and-feel. Also check that the different characters and font types can be stored in the local database.

The same applies to date formats that are used within apps. Depending on the country or region in question, different date formats are also used. You need to check that the correct format is shown depending on the region settings of the phone. You should also test the parsing from one date format to another.

The following date formats are commonly used:

- DD/MM/YYYY (Day/Month/Year)
- DD.MM.YYYY
- DD-MM-YYYY
- MM/DD/YYYY (Month/Day/Year)
- MM.DD.YYYY
- MM-DD-YYYY
- YYYY/MM/DD (Year/Month/Day)
- YYYY.MM.DD
- YYYY-MM-DD

If your app is going to be used in different countries or regions in the world, make sure you add the important languages based on your target customer group in order to provide a good user experience. When testing the app, you need to check it in every language. You also need to check that the language switch is working to be sure that only a single language is shown depending on the device's language settings. Also check the fallback language of your app. To test this, change the device language to one that is not supported and check that the app uses the implemented fallback language. Languages and date formats should never be mixed up within the app. If you want to test if the used language is correct, you should ask a native speaker in order to avoid using misleading translations or text that is simply wrong.

Important   The different languages and date formats must be considered during the design phase of the app so that designers can plan the look-and-feel of the app in all of the provided languages. Late changes due to translation issues can delay the release date of the app or negatively affect the app's design.

Mobile Browsers

If you're testing a mobile Web app, you will of course need to do so in a mobile Web browser. Mobile Web browsers are optimized to display Web content such that they can be accessed on smaller screens. Unfortunately, there is more than one mobile Web browser available in different versions of the different mobile platforms. Besides that, the browsers use different layout engines such as the following:

- Blink (www.chromium.org/blink)
- Gecko (https://developer.mozilla.org/en-US/docs/Mozilla/Gecko)
- Presto (www.opera.com/docs/specs/)
- Trident (http://msdn.microsoft.com/en-us/library/aa741312(v=vs.85) .aspx)
- WebKit (www.webkit.org/)

Depending on the layout engine, browser settings, and browser version, mobile Web apps may look and behave very differently. This is especially the case for the different browser layout engines. Every browser layout engine handles standards like HTML, CSS, and JavaScript differently. Not every browser has implemented the complete feature set or the latest version of the various languages (HTML, CSS, JavaScript), which can lead to differences in behavior.

To be sure that your mobile Web app works on different browsers, test it on different mobile platforms such as Android, iOS, Windows Phone, or Black-Berry together with different browser versions. This is of course the same problem native apps have: fragmentation. However, testing mobile Web apps can be more difficult because now you have another variable added to your testing matrix: the different Web browsers. This means that you have to focus on the different browser versions, mobile platforms, and operating system versions.

The mobile Web browsers listed in Table 3.2 are available for the different mobile platforms. To see which browser layout engine is used by which browser version, check the browser vendor Web sites.

> **Important** Not every browser is available on every platform. Table 3.2 shows the most used mobile Web browsers.[8] The table is not complete.

---

8. http://akamai.me/1EQZbP0

Table 3.2 *Overview of Mobile Browsers*

Browser	Creator	Layout Engine	Available for
Chrome (www.google.com/intl/en/chrome/browser/mobile/)	Google	WebKit (iOS), Blink	Android, iOS
Safari (https://developer.apple.com/safari/)	Apple	WebKit	iOS
Internet Explorer Mobile (http://windows.microsoft.com/en-us/internet-explorer/browser-ie#touchweb=touchvidtab1)	Microsoft	Trident	Windows Phone
BlackBerry (http://us.blackberry.com/devices/features/getting-started.html)	Research in Motion	WebKit	BlackBerry
Android Browser	Different	WebKit	Android
Dolphin Browser (http://dolphin.com/)	MoboTap	WebKit	Android, iOS
Firefox Mobile (www.mozilla.org/en-US/firefox/android/)	Mozilla	Gecko	Android
Opera Mobile (www.opera.com/mobile)	Opera Software	Presto, Blink	Android, iOS

As you can see, testing a mobile Web app on different mobile browsers can also be a real challenge. To keep the amount of testing work needed for mobile Web browsers to a minimum, you should create mobile browser groups or add mobile browser requirements to the device groups. If you create browser groups, prioritize them based on your target customer group and only test your Web app within these groups.

Summary

Chapter 3 was one of the first hands-on chapters of this book. You are now able to create your own personas based on the information about your target customer group and the usage of your app. Those personas will help you to focus your development and testing efforts on your target group and not waste time on unnecessary features.

In addition to personas, you now know how to handle device fragmentation in the mobile world. Testing your app on every mobile device is not possible or economical. Based on your target group, you can define so-called mobile device groups to test only on the devices within each group. This will help you to downsize the testing effort dramatically. Another approach to handling device fragmentation is to use mobile device labs.

As you know, mobile devices are packed with lots of sensors and interfaces, and if your app uses them, you need to test them as well. Testing the different sensors and interfaces was another big topic in this chapter. For each sensor and interface, testing ideas were provided.

When your app is available in different countries and supports different languages, the section "Internationalization (I18n) and Localization (L10n)" should help you remember to test your app against those languages and settings related to locations from around the world.

The chapter closed with an overview of the different mobile browsers that are currently available on the market.

Chapter 4

How to Test Mobile Apps

In the previous three chapters you learned a lot about the mobile app world, ranging from the different network types, app types, business models, app stores, customer expectations, and challenges for mobile testers to device-specific hardware elements. In this chapter you will learn how to test mobile apps. This is a hands-on chapter, and I suggest that you have at least one device with an app of your choice next to you while reading it.

Use your newly acquired knowledge to test the app and see if you can find bugs or other discrepancies.

Emulator, Simulator, or Real Device?

Before you start to test an app, there's one important question to answer: Are you going to test it on a real device, in a simulator, or in an emulator?

Mobile device emulators, such as the Android Emulator,[1] are desktop applications that translate the instructions of the compiled app source code so that the app can be executed on a desktop computer. The emulator acts exactly like the mobile device hardware and operating system, thus allowing the developer and tester to debug or test the application. Since the app is executed on a computer, not all of the mobile-specific hardware elements such as the sensors or touch gestures can be emulated. However, emulators can be very useful at an early stage of the development process in order to obtain quick feedback about the implemented features.

---

1. http://developer.android.com/tools/help/emulator.html

Simulators, such as the iOS simulator,[2] are less complex software applications that simulate a small subset of the device's behavior and hardware. In contrast to emulators, simulators are only similar to the target platform and simulate the real device's hardware, making them much faster than emulators. It is also not possible to test device-specific hardware elements with simulators. However, simulators are useful at an early stage of the development process in order to obtain feedback about the implemented features.

The biggest difference between a simulator and an emulator is that a simulator attempts to duplicate the behavior of the mobile device, while an emulator tries to duplicate the entire inner architecture of the mobile device and is therefore closer to the target platform. Depending on the mobile platform, vendors provide either a simulator or an emulator. Apple and BlackBerry (Research in Motion) offer a simulator; Google and Microsoft provide an emulator.

As you have learned in the previous chapters, mobile testing requires movement and different hardware, meaning that you need to test your app on physical devices to be sure that everything works together in real-life situations.

Emulators and simulators should be used only for very basic tests such as simple functionality (is the button clickable?) or to make sure the look-and-feel of the app is OK.

Manual Testing versus Automated Testing

There's another important decision to make: Are you going to test the app purely with automated tests, purely with manual tests, or with a combination of both? This decision depends on your app.

Simply performing test automation will not work and is not sufficient for several reasons. Not every mobile-device-specific function can be automated—for example, location data—and other environmental sensor data is really hard to test in a lab situation. Because of these limitations, your app will most likely contain lots of bugs and problems that your customers will find.

Only performing manual testing can work, but it's also not sufficient. You should perform only manual tests of your app if it meets the following criteria:

- Your app is very simple and basic.
- Your app has only very limited functionality.
- Your app is available for only a limited time in the app stores.

---

2. https://developer.apple.com/library/ios/documentation/IDEs/Conceptual/iOS_Simulator_Guide/Introduction/Introduction.html

In all other cases you should combine manual and automated testing. Before performing test automation, you should always do manual testing. Every new feature must be manually tested systematically on different devices. Once you've completed manual testing, you can then define the parts of the app that require test automation.

In Chapter 5, "Mobile Test Automation and Tools," I describe the different mobile test automation concepts, explain how to select a mobile test automation tool, and provide you with an overview of possible tools.

"Traditional" Testing

Mobile applications are software applications. Besides testing the mobile-specific functions and elements, it is still necessary to test mobile apps in the same way you test Web or desktop applications. You still need to design the test cases, manage the test data, and of course run the tests.

If you look at Figure 4.1, you can see the typical actions/steps that should be taken during the software quality assurance process. There are two types of software quality assurance measures: product focus and process focus. The product focus phase is used to find bugs, whereas the process focus phase aims to protect the software from bugs.

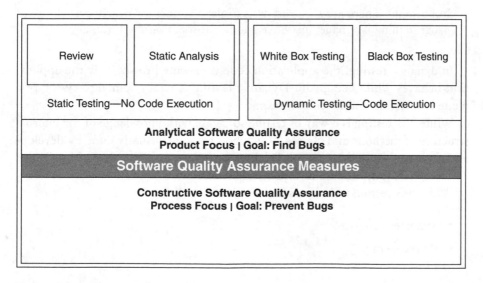

Figure 4.1 *Software quality assurance measures*

The process focus phase of software quality assurance covers the methods, languages, tools, guidelines, standards, and processes with which the software is developed. In this phase, software testers are responsible for making sure, for example, that the guidelines, development methods, and tools as well as the standards are met during the whole development process. They should guide and help developers and other team members in fulfilling the defined processes in order to prevent any bugs from arising.

The product focus phase is divided into static testing and dynamic testing.

In static testing, the software is not executed. Testers and developers should perform reviews during this stage of the software development process, either code reviews before committing the code to a repository or reviewing the documents and specifications before development starts. During the static phase, the application code will be checked with tools to see if it matches coding guidelines or contains any memory leaks or race conditions.

The following list contains some Java static analysis tools:

- Checkstyle (http://checkstyle.sourceforge.net/)
- FindBugs (http://findbugs.sourceforge.net/)
- Lint (http://tools.android.com/recent/lint)
- PMD (http://pmd.sourceforge.net/)

Important   There are static analysis tools available for nearly every programming language, just have a look for them on the Internet.

In dynamic testing, the application code is executed to see how the application behaves while being run. Dynamic testing is again split into two types: white box testing and black box testing.

White box testing is a way of testing software with knowledge of the internal structure of methods and classes. White box testing is usually done by developers who test their code on a unit level, in most cases using tools such as JUnit,[3] TestNG,[4] XCTest,[5] or similar unit testing tools.

White box testing techniques include the following:

- Statement coverage
- Path coverage

---

3. http://junit.org/
4. http://testng.org/doc/index.html
5. https://developer.apple.com/library/prerelease/ios/documentation/DeveloperTools/Conceptual/ testing_with_xcode/Introduction/Introduction.html

- Branch coverage
- Decision coverage
- Control flow testing
- Data flow testing

Black box testing is a way of testing software without any knowledge of the internal structure of the methods or classes. This approach is usually done by software testers who need to know what the software should do and don't need to know how the software actually does it. Writing test cases and planning testing activities are important parts of black box testing. There are test design techniques that should be considered in order to develop the right test cases, for example, boundary values, decision tables, and equivalence class partitioning.

Boundary value testing was developed from the experience that bugs occur on the boundaries and edges of conditions and lists. These bugs may cause the software to crash, freeze, or behave incorrectly.

Decision tables will help you to split complex applications and conditions into smaller sections, which prevents you from forgetting important features. They help you obtain an overview of the critical elements of the feature set.

Equivalence class partitioning is a technique used to define test cases that uncover error classes. Equivalence class partitioning helps you reduce the number of test cases that need to be developed during your testing activities. This approach is typically used to test possible inputs of the application.

More examples of black box testing techniques follow:

- Cause-effect graph
- Error guessing
- State transition analysis
- All-pairs testing
- Exploratory testing

Important This section gives just a very brief overview of possible testing methods and techniques. I roughly summarized the foundations of software testing and analysis, so if you're not familiar with the different test techniques, methods, and approaches, I highly recommend that you read some software testing books or take a testing class such as ISTQB[6] foundation level or Black Box Software Testing.[7]

---

6. www.istqb.org/
7. www.testingeducation.org/BBST/

Mobile-Specific Testing

In this part of the chapter you will learn how to test your app in different categories and ensure that it is robust, stable, usable, and as free of bugs as possible. Please use the knowledge you gained in Chapter 3, "Challenges in Mobile Testing," as well when testing your app. Keep the sensors, networks, gestures, customers, languages, and system apps in mind.

Before you continue reading, get your mobile device out of your pocket and start an app so that you can try out the things you're about to read.

Mobile Functional Testing

Testing the functionality of your app should be the first thing you do. Execute the designed test cases with your mobile app to make sure that the features and requirements have been correctly implemented. Besides testing your test cases, it is important that you also test the defined acceptance criteria.

Test to make sure that all the functions perform as they should, for example, inputs, outputs, tappable buttons, navigation, and data processing. Test the functionality in different mobile user scenarios and environments. Keep the sensors and interfaces of a mobile device in mind while testing the functionality (see Chapter 3 again).

Furthermore, use the quality assurance measures to test the functionality of your app in a static and dynamic way.

> **Important**   Testing the functionality is one of the most important aspects of every software project. Depending on your app, functional testing will be different in every project.

Mobile Usability Testing

Usability, especially mobile usability, is a huge, complex, and important topic. Within your mobile development team you should have a usability expert who covers this part of the development process. Good usability requires lots of refining, intense user research, and even more testing with real users. It is important that your app be easy to use; otherwise it might end up with low ratings, which cause damage to the app's and possibly your company's reputation. To avoid such reputation damage, mobile testers can perform the actions described in this part of the chapter in order to help the team develop a usable app (keep KIFSU in mind).

The following links are a good starting point if you want to learn more about mobile usability:

- Usability heuristics (www.nngroup.com/articles/ten-usability-heuristics/)

- Mobile usability (www.nngroup.com/articles/mobile-usability-update/)

- Google Best Practices (www.google.com/think/multiscreen/#mobile-best-practices)

- Usability principles and techniques (www.usability.gov/what-and-why/index.html)

- Mobile user interface and usability design principles (www.neobytesolutions.com/mobile-user-interface-and-usability-design-principles/)

Or you can refer to the following book:

- *Mobile Usability* by Raluca Budiu and Jakob Nielsen (www.nngroup.com/books/mobile-usability/)

Less Is More

When testing the usability of an app, the design principle "Less is more" is a good starting point. Check the app for useless navigation elements and buttons. If you find any, talk to your team or the usability expert and get them removed. The same applies to text and words. Remove them if they are not required to interact with the app. Try to focus on the primary content of the app. Keep the goal and the problem the app should solve in mind, and get rid of anything that is distracting.

Self-Explanatory

Check if the app is self-explanatory. Ask yourself these questions: Is the user able to see the elements with which he or she can interact? Is every element on the screen clear and understandable? This aspect of usability testing gets more difficult over time because the more you work with the app, the more blind you will become to things that are not self-explanatory. You will most likely be used to potential usability issues. In that case it makes sense to ask colleagues not involved in the app development process or your customers for early feedback.

Pay Attention to Patterns

Every app should follow a usability and design pattern. If such a pattern is in place, verify that your app follows those rules. If there is no pattern available, keep an eye on the look-and-feel of the app. Same type-elements such as buttons or text labels should have the same spacings, sizes, and colors. Check that all of the elements are accessible, for example, that buttons can also be tapped by a person with thicker fingers and on different screen sizes and densities. Also check the default patterns that are provided by the mobile platforms as your app should at least follow those patterns.

Allow Mistakes

In order to provide a truly usable app, your app must allow users to make mistakes. If a user, for example, misses a required input field, provide friendly and useful error messages. Check that the error messages are not too generic and that they describe the error in a way that people without a technical background can easily understand. Furthermore, nice error highlighting should be in place to show the user the mistake he or she made. Keep your target customer group in mind when verifying error messages as this will have an impact on the wording. Besides that, your app should provide undo and go back actions in order to offer the user an easy way to correct errors. Another approach may involve user input recommendations or so-called type-ahead searches, which provide the user with possible input solutions; for example, when he or she is typing "New Y," the app will suggest New York as a possible input.

Check Workflows, Details, and Navigation

If your app follows a special workflow, check that it follows the same workflow in every section. Keep an eye on the details of those workflows. Be sure that buttons, labels, and other elements are big or small enough to be used. Screen division is important, so check the app on smaller and bigger screens. Don't forget to check the app for important details. Are they prominent enough? Is the user able to find them? Also keep an eye on visual transitions such as animations or elements that fade in or out. Is the transition of those elements smooth or does it feel choppy? Make sure you also use slow devices to check that all of your animations are smooth enough.

Check that the main navigation and sub-navigation of the app are easy to use. Are there any unnecessary taps that the user must perform in order to reach his or her goal? Check that the navigation has no unnecessary steps, and check to see if some of the steps can be combined. Is the navigation doable with one hand? Ask people who have different hand sizes and are left- or right-handed to perform this task. Have the platform-specific navigation patterns been met?

Check the Wording

Verify that the text used within the app is clear and easy to understand. Ask different people if they understand the wording and the feature behind it. If your app contains text, it must be free of typos as they can be very embarrassing and have an impact on your store reviews and ratings as well as your reputation. If your app supports more than one language, be sure the text fits into every UI element and that the translation is correct. Don't forget to test your app for placeholder texts like "Lorem ipsum" or any other default texts from developers or designers.

Check Consistency

A really important task within mobile usability testing is to check for consistency. Verify that your app is consistent in every section or view. As I already mentioned, the UI elements must have the same look-and-feel, the same text, spacings, colors, and images. Furthermore, it is really important to check that your app is consistent over all of the supported mobile platforms such as iOS, Android, Windows Phone, or BlackBerry, not just in terms of navigation or patterns (each mobile platform has its own rules), but by ensuring that the texts, colors, and images are the same. Make sure you also check the consistency of any offered Web or desktop applications that provide a different view to your application.

All of your applications must follow the corporate identity guidelines of your company in order to lend a familiar look-and-feel to your product; otherwise the user may get confused. Ask for your corporate identity guidelines, which will include topics such as colors, fonts, logos, images, and text.

Write It Down

While testing your app, it is important that you write down everything that feels different or somehow jumps out at you, no matter how trivial it may seem. Detailed observations are really important and will help improve the app. You can create screenshots of the entire screen using the mobile-platform-specific button combination or screen capture videos with a Web cam while using the app to show these "wrong" things to your product owner or developer so that you can discuss them.

An important point is: don't give up writing down such things, even if the product owner or the developer rejects your findings time and time again. Fight for those things and keep raising them. However, do be careful with your bug reminders as it is likely that your complaints will be ignored if you constantly raise the same issues. I suggest that you collect and categorize rejected bugs and present them as an improvement story to your product manager or developer for one of the next releases. Another approach would be to include fixes of old bugs in every release to improve the mobile app and clean up the bug pool. Talk to your team and find the solution that works best with your app.

Testers need to be curious and tenacious, and your customers will love you for that!

Accessibility Testing

As you have learned from the previous chapters, lots of people around the world are using mobile devices and mobile apps in their daily life. Apps are used for a whole range of different reasons, such as navigation, hotel bookings, ticket purchases, listening to music, or playing games.

When developing and testing an app, did you think about people with disabilities?

There are many people out there who are visually, audibly, physically, and/or cognitively impaired. Making mobile apps accessible is not easy and it's a lot of work, but it doesn't just benefit people with disabilities; it also improves your company's reputation and increases your user base.

It is therefore very important that everyone involved in your mobile app development process be aware of accessibility and know about the accessibility requirements of mobile apps. There are four types of impairment that are relevant to mobile app development: visual, auditory, physical, and cognitive.

Visual Impairment

People with visual impairment may be blind, have limited vision, be color-blind, or have a color deficiency. Due to their visual impairment, they may not be able to see all of the buttons, labels, text, and other elements in your app and are therefore unable to access or control the app correctly.

To adapt your mobile app for visually impaired people, you can implement the following features:

- Make all elements available for screen readers. Nearly every mobile platform offers the option to use a built-in screen reader to read out the content and the elements of the mobile app. If there are no built-in screen readers available, you can install them from third-party vendors.

- Every mobile platform offers a built-in feature to enlarge the font size of the entire phone and apps. Implement your app in such a way that the font size can be adjusted while retaining a pleasant layout.

- Every mobile platform offers a feature to change the foreground or background color of the screen, or to change the contrast. Therefore, you should use colors, brightness, and contrast of the UI elements that work with the different foreground and background settings.

- Built-in screen magnifiers can be used to enlarge the elements on the screen to make them easier to read.

- Another way of helping visually impaired people is through the use of voice recognition. This allows mobile users to control the entire mobile app through voice commands.

Auditory Impairment

Some people have trouble hearing, meaning that they don't hear if someone calls them or if they receive audio notifications, instructions, or any other kind of audio content.

To help people with hearing problems, you can do the following:

- Use the built-in vibration or visual notification to inform users when they receive a call, message, or any other notification.

- If your app relies on video content, use subtitles to inform the user about the content of the video.

- Implement adjustable sound or volume controls. This is really important for people with a hearing aid.

- If your app generates any sounds, implement a feature to switch the device to mono audio. This will help people who can hear with only one ear.

Physical Impairment

Physically impaired people have problems performing gestures with their hands. They are not able to use gestures such as pinch, tap, or swipe to control the elements on the phone or within the mobile app.

To help them use your app, you can do the following things:

- Use voice recognition as this allows mobile users to control the entire mobile app through voice commands.

- Implement a feature to increase or decrease the speed of pressing buttons as this will make it easier for physically impaired people to control your app.

Cognitive Impairment

Cognitively impaired people may have problems related to attention, communication, memory, computation, and reading skills. Those people experience problems, for example, with understanding complex navigations or instructions that they need to follow within an application.

To help them use your app, you can do the following things:

- Implement an easy and intuitive user interface. Make it as simple as possible to understand and use.

- Use screen readers in combination with simultaneous text highlighting.

- Implement an auto-text feature for input fields so that preloaded and defined text elements are already in place.

- Implement your app in such a way that cognitively impaired people have enough time to complete an operation.

Accessibility Guidelines

As you have seen, accessibility testing is a really challenging task, and you and your team need to find a way to support such features. If your app is accessible, it is very important that you test it with people who have such impairments in order to be sure that the requirements have been correctly implemented. Providing an accessible app will increase your user base and improve your reputation.

The W3C created an accessibility initiative that covers most of the accessibility concerns. You can find information at www.w3.org/WAI/ or www.w3.org/WAI/mobile/. To get detailed mobile accessibility information for the different mobile platforms, check the manufacturers' Web pages.

The guidelines for Android can be found here:

- Android accessibility guide (http://developer.android.com/guide/topics/ui/accessibility/index.html)

- Android accessibility testing (http://developer.android.com/tools/testing/testing_accessibility.html)

The guidelines for iOS can be found here:

- iOS accessibility introduction (https://developer.apple.com/library/ios/documentation/UserExperience/Conceptual/iPhoneAccessibility/Introduction/Introduction.html)

- Accessibility on iPhone (https://developer.apple.com/library/ios/documentation/UserExperience/Conceptual/iPhoneAccessibility/Accessibility_on_iPhone/Accessibility_on_iPhone.html)

- iOS accessibility testing (https://developer.apple.com/library/ios/technotes/TestingAccessibilityOfiOSApps/TestingtheAccessibilityofiOSApps/TestingtheAccessibilityofiOSApps.html)

The guidelines for Windows Phone can be found here:

- Windows Phone accessibility guide (www.windowsphone.com/en-us/how-to/wp8/settings-and-personalization/accessibility-on-my-phone)

The guidelines for BlackBerry are here:

- BlackBerry accessibility guide (http://ca.blackberry.com/legal/accessibility.html)

Battery Usage Testing

While testing a mobile app, you need to test battery consumption during use. If your app consumes too much power, users will delete it and move on to another one.

To test your app's battery usage, you can run through the two scenarios described in the following sections.

Fully Charged Battery

In the first scenario, you have a fully charged battery. After installing and starting the app, leave it open and put the device in standby mode (your app is now running in the foreground). Now you have to wait a couple of minutes (or hours) to see whether the app is consuming lots of battery. Check the battery usage from time to time and note the battery level. You should do this with different devices to get better results, and don't forget to close any other apps that are running on the device to eliminate any side effects they may cause. The same test should be done when the app is running in the background. To put the app in the background, just start it and then close it (by pressing the home button or close button). On most mobile platforms, the app will now run in the background or multitask mode. Again, check the device from time to time to monitor the app's battery usage.

Use the smartphone hardware features (if used within your app) such as GPS or other sensors and check the battery level of your device while using those features. It's important that your app switch off device features once they are no longer needed. If your app doesn't do this, it will consume lots of battery. Check that the app is not sending any unnecessary requests to a backend system while running in the background or foreground. Unnecessary requests will have an impact on battery life. To check this, use a proxy tool such as Charles[8] or

---

8. www.charlesproxy.com/

Fiddler[9] to send all your requests and communications from the device through your workstation to the backend system.

While using the device and the app, check to see if the device gets hot. In some cases device-specific features will cause the device and battery to heat up, which will have an impact on your device hardware and may ultimately damage it.

Also check that your app really is closed after removing it from the multitask thread. To verify this, open the mobile-specific app system settings and check that your app is not currently running there.

Low Battery

The second scenario you should test is when the battery of the phone is nearly empty, when it has 10% to 15% of its capacity left. In this battery state, most mobile devices switch off features such as network connections, GPS, and sensors in order to prolong the battery life. If your app uses any of those features, check how it handles this low battery state. Watch out for freezes, crashes, and performance issues.

On some devices you can activate a power-saving mode that switches off sensors or Internet connections. Again, don't forget to check how your app handles this power-saving mode.

A really important test is to see how your app handles a completely empty battery. Use your app until the phone battery dies. Then plug in a charger and start the phone again. Once the phone has booted up, check your app for data loss or data corruption. The app should work as expected and no data loss or corruption should occur.

You should also test your app in the transition from a good to a bad battery state. Most devices will pop up an alert informing the user that the battery is nearly empty. This transition can have an impact on your app, so check it for freezes, crashes, and performance issues. The same should be done the other way around. Use your app while the battery is charging as this can also impact the app.

Battery Consumption Tools

Some mobile platforms offer a battery usage statistic to see which app is consuming the most battery. Android, for example, provides such an overview to see the current state of the battery (see Figure 4.2). Use this tool for your battery state testing; it's really useful for mobile testers!

---

9. www.telerik.com/fiddler

Figure 4.2 *Android app battery usage overview*

If you or your developers want to constantly measure battery consumption during your project, there are tools available for that. For Android there is a tool called JouleUnit.[10] JouleUnit is an open-source energy profiling tool for Android apps that finds any unnecessary battery usage of apps when they are running. It also measures the usage of the CPU, Wi-Fi, or display brightness. The tool basically has the same structure as JUnit tests and is really easy to integrate within your development environment so you can get early feedback about the battery consumption of your app.

iOS allows you to use the energy usage function within Instruments[11] to profile the energy usage of your app. Instruments is part of the Xcode development environment and is free for testers and developers.

There are a couple of useful documents online about energy usage within Instruments:

- Energy Usage Instrument
  (https://developer.apple.com/library/ios/documentation/AnalysisTools/
  Reference/Instruments_User_Reference/EnergyUsageInstrument/Energy-
  UsageInstrument.html)

---

10. https://code.google.com/p/jouleunit/
11. https://developer.apple.com/library/mac/documentation/developertools/conceptual/instruments
    userguide/Introduction/Introduction.html

- Logging energy usage in iOS
  (https://developer.apple.com/library/ios/recipes/Instruments_help_articles/
  LoggingEnergyUsageinaniOSDevice/LoggingEnergyUsageinaniOSDevice
  .html)

Battery testing is easy to do and should be part of your tool chain. Combine the manual with the profiling approach to get good results.

Stress and Interrupt Testing

Stress and interrupt testing is an important part of the mobile testing process. With the aid of tools, mobile testers are able to determine any potential performance or stability issues exhibited by an app. To test your app against interrupts, you can manually trigger lots of notifications to the device while using the app. Notifications can be incoming messages, calls, app updates, or push notifications (software interrupts). Furthermore, pressing the volume up and down buttons or any other kind of hardware button is also an interrupt (hardware interrupt) that can also have an impact on your app.

Doing all of these tasks manually is a lot of work and very time-consuming. In most cases, these test scenarios can't be done manually because it is very hard to simulate fast and multiple user inputs with one or two hands. But it can be done with the aid of tools, and it is really easy to integrate them into the development and testing process.

For Android apps, a tool called Monkey[12] can be used which is part of the Android SDK (Software Development Kit). Monkey can run on either a physical device or an emulator. While running, it generates pseudo-random user events such as a touch, click, rotate, swipe, mute, Internet connection shutdown, and much more to stress-test the app and see how it handles all those inputs and interrupts.

The package name of the Android .apk file is needed to be able to run Monkey; otherwise it will execute its random commands to the entire phone instead of just the app under test.

With access to the app code, the package name can be found in the AndroidManifest.xml. If only the compiled .apk file is available, mobile testers can use the Android Asset Packaging Tool[13] (aapt) to get the package name from the app. aapt is located in the build-tools folder of the installed Android SDK version.

---

12. http://developer.android.com/tools/help/monkey.html
13. http://elinux.org/Android_aapt

The path to aapt may look like this:

```
/../daniel/android/sdk/build-tools/android-4.4/
```

With the following command, the package name can be read out from the .apk file:

```
./aapt d badging /daniel/myApp/myApp.apk | grep 'pack'
...
package: name='com.myApp' versionCode='' versionName=''
...
```

When the package name (in this case `com.myApp`) is available, execute Monkey with adb[14] (Android Debug Bridge):

```
./adb shell monkey -p com.myApp -v 2000
```

The number 2000 indicates the number of random commands that Monkey will perform. With an additional parameter `-s` for seed, Monkey will generate the same sequence of events again. This is really important for reproducing a bug that may occur when running Monkey.

For iOS apps there is a similar tool called UI AutoMonkey.[15] UI AutoMonkey is also able to generate multiple commands to stress-test an iOS app. To use UI AutoMonkey, a UIAutomation Instruments template must be configured within Xcode. After the template is configured, a JavaScript file needs to be written to tell the tool how many and which commands should be executed during the stress testing session (see Listing 4.1).

Listing 4.1 *UI AutoMonkey Script*

```
config: {
  numberOfEvents: 2000,
  delayBetweenEvents: 0.05,     // In seconds

  // Events that will be triggered on the phone
  eventWeights: {
    tap: 30,
    drag: 1,
    flick: 1,
    orientation: 1,
    clickVolumeUp: 1,
```

---

14. http://developer.android.com/tools/help/adb.html
15. https://github.com/jonathanpenn/ui-auto-monkey

```
    clickVolumeDown: 1,
    lock: 1,
    pinchClose: 10,
    pinchOpen: 10,
    shake: 1
  },

// Probability that touch events will have these different properties
  touchProbability: {
    multipleTaps: 0.05,
    multipleTouches: 0.05,
    longPress: 0.05
  }
},
```

If the script is written, it can be executed within Xcode. At the end, both tools generate an overview of possible errors and problems within the app.

> **Important**   Please visit the tool manufacturer's Web site for installation instructions.

As you can see, these tools make it simple to stress- and interrupt-test a mobile application. Besides that, using them is a huge benefit for mobile testers as it helps the team build a reliable and robust mobile app. By the way, it's useful to combine battery testing with stress and interrupt testing to see how the battery is used when lots of interrupts and user inputs are triggered throughout the app.

Performance Testing

Performance testing is one of the key testing areas in every software development project and especially for mobile apps. If you remember the high user expectations described in Chapter 1, "What's Special about Mobile Testing?," mobile performance testing is a really important and critical part of app development. Mobile users expect an app to start/load within two seconds; otherwise they are unhappy and may delete it.

Testers and developers can use performance tests to discover potential bottlenecks in their software application. Normally, performance testing is done on servers or backend systems to check how the systems or software can handle huge numbers of requests, to meet acceptable results for the users.

Performance tests must be executed in a defined state of the application with hardware resources that are equal to the live backend environment. The collected data must then be analyzed to find possible bottlenecks and problems in the software. Performance testing is a complex topic that should never be underestimated or postponed to the end of the project; it should be done as early as possible. Key performance figures should be part of the requirements phase of app development in order to start planning right from the beginning.

For mobile apps, performance tests are more complex and need to cover more systems in order to get meaningful results that improve performance.

The typical mobile app relies on a backend system (server) with which it communicates. The app sends requests to the server, which then handles those requests and sends back a response. To send a simple request to a backend system, there are three critical performance areas that need to be covered:

- The server
- The mobile data networks
- The mobile device and app itself

To test the performance of mobile apps, you need to performance-test at least the backend system and the app itself. It is not possible to test the performance of the mobile data networks, and it makes no sense for you as a mobile tester. The network speed and latency can be simulated during the testing phase, but the network speed will be totally different while a user is on the move in real data networks.

In this chapter, I want to focus on performance testing of the mobile app itself. Keep the backend system performance in mind and look for further information on the Internet. There are plenty of good tools available to help you set up a performance testing suite. If you want to do performance testing within your project and use tools to do so, keep the following steps in mind as they will help you to define a clear strategy:

1. Plan performance tests early in the development phase.

2. Design the performance tests for your app.

3. Prepare test data and infrastructure (these should be the same as for the live environment).

4. Execute the performance tests.

5. Collect, analyze, and evaluate the data.

6. Find potential bottlenecks and refine the app.

7. Monitor the application changes again to see if the refinements were good enough.

Mobile App Performance Testing

When testing the performance of a mobile app, keep it simple and focus on the UI of the app. For example, use a stopwatch and measure the application launch or the delays between certain operations. Measure the loading time of the content such as images, text, or animations that need to be created or processed by the app. Perform those tests several times and note the performed steps in order to reproduce and track possible performance issues. Also, write down how often the problem occurred. If it happens all the time, that's fine; that is an easy fix. But some problems, especially performance problems, may happen only three out of ten times. It's therefore important to find the bug and reproduce the behavior.

While testing the app, write down everything that seems slow as it could be a potential performance issue. Manual performance testing should be done on several devices with different hardware specifications in order to get meaningful results.

Another test that should be done is a comparison between the current app version that is live and available for download in the app stores and the new release candidate app. Compare both versions in terms of app launch time and all other areas. The new release candidate should not be slower than the current version; otherwise the app will get bad feedback from users.

> **Important**   The comparison should be done on the same hardware; otherwise the results will differ.

If your app contains third-party elements such as advertising or news feeds, check that those elements have no impact on the performance of the app. As an example, you can use a Web proxy tool like Fiddler to send the third-party request to a time-out to see that it has no impact on the app's performance.

Another way to test the performance of the app is to profile and measure the process and operation time of the code. There are plenty of profiler tools available to check the app code for potential bottlenecks and performance issues. This task should be done by the developers, so encourage them to use such tools.

To summarize the simple mobile app performance tests:

- Measure the app's launch time.
- Check for delays during operations or user interactions.
- Measure the loading time of the content.
- Note everything that seems slow.

- Test on different hardware, especially on slower phones.
- Compare the live app version with the new release candidate.
- Check for third-party elements.
- Use profiling tools to measure the process and operation time of methods and classes.

As you can see, these are simple steps to test the performance of a mobile app. If you want more complex and detailed data about the performance of the app, the backend, and the data networks, you'll need to use a performance testing tool or solution that covers all parts. There are plenty of mobile app performance providers available, so search for them on the Internet and see which one best fits your development and test environment.

Standby Testing

Standby testing is really easy and simple to do but can show some nice crashes, freezes, and UI glitches within the app. While the app is running, put the device into standby mode by pressing the off button once. Depending on the app under test, wake up the device after a couple of seconds, minutes, or hours to see how the app reacts upon wake-up. Most apps fetch data updates from the backend system after a wake-up to refresh the current UI. It's possible for a bug to prevent the app from displaying the newly fetched data correctly, or it may freeze or crash. If a UI view update mechanism is implemented, you must make sure this mechanism works after the device wakes up and fetches the latest data.

Also test the scenario of not having an Internet connection while the app is in standby mode. To test that, open the app, close the device's Internet connection, and put the device into standby. After a certain amount of time, wake up the device and check the behavior of the app. It will probably check for updates, but there is no Internet connection. In this case, the app must show a proper error message to the user, informing him or her of the current situation.

Don't forget to check that the device is able to communicate with device-specific hardware elements after waking up. Feel free to get creative when testing the app for standby and wake-up problems.

Installation Testing

The installation process is the first impression a mobile customer has of an app. If the installation fails due to errors or problems, the customer will not try to download the app again and will move on to another one. To avoid such problems, installation testing must be made part of the mobile testing process and should be performed at least before a new version is due for release.

To test your app for installation problems, perform the following tasks:

- Verify that the app can be installed successfully on the local storage or memory card of the device.
- Check that the installation works with different Internet connections such as Wi-Fi or mobile data networks.
- Change the Internet connection (Wi-Fi to 3G, for example) while the app is installing.
- Switch to other apps while the app is installing.
- Switch the device's Internet connection off, for example, to airplane mode, while the app is installing.
- Try to install the app when there is not enough space left on the local storage.
- Try to install the app via data cable or syncing from mobile-specific software applications.

When performing those actions, watch out for error messages in the app as well as crashes and freezes.

When the app successfully installs, mobile testers should also test the other way around by testing the uninstall process. So uninstall the app and check that it is completely removed from the device with no data left on the hardware or local storage. To verify that the app was removed completely, check the device's memory and folders for leftover data. Another way to verify that the app was removed successfully is to install the app again and to check that, say, a user is not logged in automatically or that the app doesn't show any data from the previous installation. These tests are really important because some devices are shared within a company or family and leftover data can lead to serious trouble.

Some mobile platforms offer different ways of uninstalling an app, so you have to test all of them. While uninstalling the app, watch out for error messages, crashes, and freezes.

Update Testing

As you have learned in the previous sections, testing an app during the install and uninstall processes is really important. Besides installing and uninstalling an app, users are also able to update the app from one version to another. During this update process, lots of things can go wrong and need to be tested before a new app version is submitted to the app stores.

Testing the update process includes scenarios such as the following:

- Logged-in users should not be logged out from the app after the update is installed.

- The update will not affect the local database; that is, existing data will not be modified or deleted.

- The app is in the same state as before the update was installed.

- Testing the update process will simulate the update process in the app stores.

You should also test the update process from a far older app version to the latest one to see what happens to the app. While doing update testing, keep an eye out for error messages, crashes, freezes, and performance issues right after the update.

In the following two sections, I will describe how to perform update testing on iOS and Android. Nevertheless, if you are testing a Windows Phone, Black-Berry, or any other kind of app, you should of course do update testing as well.

iOS Update Testing

There are two ways of simulating the update process for iOS apps. The first one can be performed with iTunes by following these steps:

1. Build an ad hoc version of the app that is currently live in the Apple App Store.
   HINT: This version must have the same bundle identifier (package name or structure of the app classes) as the new app.

2. Be sure that no older version of the app is installed within iTunes and on the test device (sync with iTunes to be sure).

3. Drag the app from step 1 into iTunes and sync the version to your test device.

4. Launch the app and do some manual testing to make sure that the app is working.

5. Build the new release candidate version of the app, drag it to iTunes, and sync it to the device. iTunes should confirm that the older version will be removed.
   HINT: Do *not* delete the old build! In the next step iTunes will install the new app over the old one and simulate the update from the App Store.

6. Launch the new version of the app and check that everything is OK.

The second way of testing the update process for iOS is to use the Apple Configurator.[16] This tool is far easier to use, especially if you want to test the update procedure on several iOS test devices such as an iPhone 4(S), iPhone 5(S), or iPad.

1. Build an ad hoc version of the app that is currently live in the Apple App Store. **HINT:** This version must have the same bundle identifier as the new app.

2. Be sure that no older version of the app is installed on the test device.

3. Use the tool to install the app from step 1 to the devices for which you want to check the update process.

4. Launch the app and do some manual testing to make sure that the app is working.

5. Build the new release candidate version of the app and install it with the tool. The update process will be simulated.

6. Launch the new version of the app and check that everything is OK.

For further information, please read the technical note TN2285[17] from Apple about testing updates on iOS devices.

Android Update Testing
The same update testing can be done with Android apps. To test the update process for Android apps, you can use the adb tool located in the Android SDK folder:

1. Install the current Google Play store version of the app to the test device:

   ```
   ./adb install RELEASED_APP_NAME.apk
   ```

2. Check that this version works.

3. Build a release candidate of the Android app. **HINT:** Be sure to sign the release candidate with the Play store keystore.

4. Use the following command to install the new version of the app and to test the update procedure:

   ```
   ./adb install -r NEW_VERSION_APP.apk
   ```

   The option -r means the app will be reinstalled and retain its data on the phone.

5. The new version of the app is now installed and can be tested.

---

16. http://help.apple.com/configurator/mac/1.7/?lang=en
17. https://developer.apple.com/library/ios/technotes/tn2285/_index.html#//apple_ref/doc/uid/ DTS40011323

As you can see, update testing is very easy to do. It's really important to perform these checks before submitting an app to the various app stores.

Database Testing

Apps use local databases, in most cases a SQLite[18] database, to persist data on the phone. Storing the data or the content of an app in a local database enables mobile apps to present the content when the device is offline. This is a huge advantage compared to mobile Web apps that rely on a stable Internet connection in order to work properly. The fact that mobile apps use databases means that mobile testers need to test them and the actions that will be executed on the database.

Local database testing can be performed manually or automated. The goal is to test data integrity while editing, deleting, or modifying the data. In order to achieve good database testing, you need to know the database model with the table names, procedures, triggers, and functions. With the help of database tools, you can connect to the device database to test and verify the data.

The following types of tests should form part of your mobile database testing:

- Database validation testing
- Database integration testing
- Database performance testing
- Procedure and function testing
- Trigger testing
- CRUD (Create/Read/Update/Delete) operations testing to make sure they will work on the database
- Testing that the database changes are shown correctly on the UI of the app
- Search and indexing function testing
- Database security testing
- Testing the database for migrations

Because databases and database testing are huge topics in themselves, I recommend further reading to gather more information about the different database technologies. The "Books about SQLite"[19] page contains lots of useful books on this topic.

---

18. www.sqlite.org/
19. www.sqlite.org/books.html

Local Storage Testing

Local storage testing has nothing to do with the app database; instead, you should check how the app reacts in different states of the device's local storage. Every device has a certain amount of storage capacity for music, images, apps, and any other kind of data that can be stored on the device. Some devices have only a single central and permanently installed local storage, and users are not able to extend those devices with additional storage. However, there are many devices that offer the possibility to extend the local storage, for example, with a microSD card.

When testing a mobile app, you should test the app together with different states of the local storage to be sure that the app can handle them properly. The following scenarios should be tested:

- Test the app when the local storage is full.
- Test the app when the local storage is full but the extended storage still has some space left.
- Test the app when the local storage has some space left but the extended storage is full.
- Test the app when both storage areas are full.
- Test the app when the local storage is nearly full. Perform some actions within the app that will write lots of data to the local storage in order to fill it up.
- Remove the device's extended storage and check the behavior of the app.
- If possible, move the app to the extended storage and check the behavior.
- Test the app when the local storage is empty.

When performing these scenarios, watch out for app crashes, error messages, app freezes, performance issues, UI glitches, and any other kind of strange behavior that could indicate a problem.

Security Testing

Security can be business critical—for example, when attackers steal your customer data—thus making it a very important part of the development and testing process of your mobile app. Security testing is a complex topic that requires knowledge in many different areas, such as client-server communication, software architecture, and system architecture. Because of its complex nature and the specialized skill set required, security testing is best done by experts. It includes methods such as manual or automated penetration testing with man-in-the-middle attacks, fuzzing, scanning, and auditing the software.

Penetration testing is an approach used to find security weaknesses in an application that allow access to its features and data. There are several open-source and enterprise tools on the market that can test the application for common vulnerabilities. A list of common security testing tools can be found on the OWASP (Open Web Application Security Project) page.[20]

With the aid of a proxy tool, an attacker can change or monitor communication between a client and a server. This allows the attacker to read sensitive data such as usernames and passwords or manipulate the behavior of the client by sending forged data to it. This method is known as a man-in-the-middle attack.

Fuzzing is a method to generate and send random data to a system in order to see how the system reacts to the data in preparation for a possible attack. Thanks to scanning tools, the system can be checked for known vulnerabilities that can be exploited in order to gain access.

Audits are most likely performed by certified security providers. With the help of the external partners, the application will be checked manually and automatically for vulnerabilities and possible attacks.

Recall that the default mobile app architecture includes the following:

- The mobile app itself
- The mobile data networks
- The backend system

You have three possible areas that need to be tested for security. It will be nigh on impossible to test the data networks for security, but the data network providers already do this to ensure a safe and secure communication environment. Therefore, two areas remain for security testing: the app and the backend. To simplify things, I want to focus on mobile app security testing.

Common App Security Mistakes

The following list contains the most common security problems of mobile apps:

> **Important**   These points can be used during the development phase to check for common mistakes. However, looking for these common mistakes is not a replacement for expert security testing like that mentioned earlier.

---

20. www.owasp.org/index.php/Appendix_A:_Testing_Tools

- **Cache storage:** Sensitive data such as passwords or tokens is cached on the device.

- **Unintended local storage:** Sensitive data such as passwords, tokens, or credit card details is stored by accident.

- **Encryption:** Sensitive data such as passwords is not encrypted on the device storage.

- **Client-side validation:** Password verification is performed only on the client side.

- **Unencrypted communication:** Communication from the app to the backend systems is not encrypted.

- **Unnecessary app permissions:** Apps use permissions for device features that they do not need or use.

To avoid these mistakes, you should keep them in mind and test for them. To verify the cache storage of the device, test your app for inputs and data that are not stored on the device. Check the device cache storage for data you just entered and verify that the data is cached for only a certain amount of time. To verify the cache storage, use an app that is able to look at the file system level and check that the cache folder of your app contains only the permitted data. Turn the device off and on again and check the device and app cache as both must be empty in order to ensure that there is no sensitive data left on the device. The same applies to data that is stored on the device by accident.

Check the device storage and files for data that is not allowed to be on the device. To verify the local storage of the device, use apps or developer tools that grant access to the local storage.

If your app uses a local database to persist the content or data such as the login credentials of your app, be sure that such data is encrypted in the local database. Check that a form of encryption is in place at the database level.

If your app uses a login to grant access to the features and content delivered from a backend system, be sure that the user is not validated on the client side. Validation should always be performed on the backend system. If the device gets lost and validation is carried out only on the client side, it is very easy for attackers to change the validation, to manipulate or steal sensitive data.

Most apps rely on a backend system for the user to send or receive information and data, to read the latest news, to communicate with friends in social networks, or to send e-mails. If the communication between the app and the backend contains sensitive, unencrypted data, it makes sense to encrypt it, such as with TLS (Transport Layer Security).

If an app wants to use a device-specific feature such as the camera or wants to synchronize contacts with the address book, special permission to access those elements is required. When developing and testing an app, keep an eye on those permissions. Use only the permissions your app really needs. Otherwise the user may not use your app, because he or she is skeptical about it or may feel like he or she is being watched. The use of unnecessary permissions can also be a vulnerability for the app and the data stored on the device. If you don't know the permissions of your app, talk to your developers about it and ask critical questions about the permissions and their purpose.

Security Requirements Analysis

The security requirements analysis should be part of the first requirements analysis phase of each mobile app project. You should raise the topic as early as possible to avoid problems at the end of the project. The following list can help you with the security requirements analysis:

- Identify the possible user roles as well as their limitations and permissions within the architecture (app and backend).

- Does the user role have an impact on the existing security, for example, the backend?

- Is an external audit required? What should be part of this audit?

- What kind of security testing approaches and tools are required in order to achieve a good security level?

- Do we have enough skills for security testing?

This list is by no means complete. Depending on the app and its complexity, this list can be much longer.

A good source of valuable information about mobile security is the "OWASP Mobile Security Project" page.[21] The project collects information about mobile security such as the following:

- Mobile Tools (www.owasp.org/index.php/OWASP_Mobile_Security_Project #tab=Mobile_Tools)

- Mobile Security Testing (www.owasp.org/index.php/OWASP_Mobile_Security_Project#tab =Mobile_Security_Testing)

- Mobile Cheat Sheet (www.owasp.org/index.php/OWASP_Mobile_Security_Project#tab =Mobile_Cheat_Sheet)

---

21. www.owasp.org/index.php/OWASP_Mobile_Security_Project

This information can be very useful during both the security requirements analysis phase and the actual security testing phase.

Another interesting and useful part of the OWASP project is the list of "Top 10 Mobile Risks."[22] The list includes the following topics, with a good explanation of each topic and possible solutions:

1. Weak Server Side Controls

2. Insecure Data Storage

3. Insufficient Transport Layer Protection

4. Unintended Data Leakage

5. Poor Authorization and Authentication

6. Broken Cryptography

7. Client Side Injection

8. Security Decisions via Untrusted Inputs

9. Improper Session Handling

10. Lack of Binary Protection

Mobile Security Testing Summary

Security testing is a complex and difficult part of the software development and testing process. It requires special skills and knowledge of technology to ensure that the software or app is secure against attacks and vulnerabilities. You as a mobile tester should always keep security testing in mind. Talk about the topic as early as possible in the requirements analysis phase. If you're not sure whether you can test the security of the app sufficiently, you should get some help from experts as early as possible in the process.

Keep the following points in mind to ensure a secure mobile app:

• Test the app for different inputs; for example, have a prepared list of possible attack strings available.

• Do penetration testing on the app and the backend system.

• Use a proxy, a fuzzer, and a scanner to verify each part of the app and the backend architecture.

---

22. www.owasp.org/index.php/OWASP_Mobile_Security_Project#tab=Top_10_Mobile_Risks

- Check the app for common mistakes.
- Have a look at the OWASP Mobile Security Project and follow the guidelines set out there.
- Check the app's certifications.
- Keep up-to-date with the latest mobile technologies and security news.
- Hire experts.

> **Important**   The security topics covered in this chapter are a very rough overview of possible things to consider. Mobile security is a huge and complex topic, so please scour the Internet for further information.

Platform Guideline Testing

Another topic you need to be aware of is the mobile-platform-specific guidelines. Each app has to follow such guidelines in order to meet the design, usability, and platform-specific patterns. If the app fails to follow these guidelines, it might be rejected from the app store. In addition, following the design principles will make your customers happy because they know how to use platform-specific features such as swiping from left to right to switch views, or to pull to refresh and update the current view.

It is important that such guidelines be included in the design phase of an app. Following the guidelines from the very beginning of the project will save you time at the end because you will encounter fewer bugs than you would by not following the guidelines.

When testing a mobile app, keep the platform-specific guidelines in mind. You should know them by heart or at least know where to find them:

- Apple iOS design resources
  (https://developer.apple.com/library/ios/design/index.html#//apple_ref/doc/uid/TP40013289)
- Apple iOS approval guidelines
  (https://developer.apple.com/appstore/resources/approval/guidelines.html)
- Android guidelines
  (https://developer.android.com/design/patterns/index.html)
- Windows Phone guidelines (http://dev.windowsphone.com/en-us/design)
- BlackBerry guidelines (http://developer.blackberry.com/design/bb10/)

> **Important**   Make sure you're familiar with the latest mobile platform guidelines. They change with every new mobile operating system version that's released.

Conformance Testing

Conformance testing aims to ensure that the software meets a defined set of standards. These standards are defined by independent entities such as the European Telecommunications Standards Institute[23] (ETSI), the World Wide Web Consortium (W3C),[24] and the Institute of Electrical and Electronics Engineers (IEEE).[25]

If your app has to implement defined standards, you must verify that those standards are met. It is important for you to be aware of those standards and that you know how to check them. However, the standards should already form part of your requirements analysis phase. When it comes to the development phase, talk to your developers about implementing the standards by asking questions, performing a code review, and walking through the defined standards documentation.

Depending on the mobile app type and purpose, an external institution may be required to verify your app in order to check that you correctly implemented their standards. This will be the case with medical apps or apps that are used by governments. In some cases, the app has to be tested for legal compliance.

> **Important**   Keep conformance testing in mind and ask questions at the very beginning of the project.

Checking the Log Files

While testing your mobile app, connect your device to your computer and check the app's log files while using it. To get access to the log files, you need to install the developer tools on your computer so you can run the app in debug mode.

When checking the log files, watch out for errors, warnings, or exceptions that occur while using the app. Save the information from the log file along with steps for how to reproduce the problem and pass the information on to the developers. Log file information is extremely useful to developers for finding

---

23. www.etsi.org/
24. www.w3.org/
25. www.ieee.org/index.html

and solving problems. Besides looking for errors and crashes, you should look for sensitive data such as tokens or passwords that are visible in the logs.

When testing your app without a cable connection to your computer, and the app crashes or exhibits strange behavior, leave the app and the device in this state and connect it as soon as possible to your computer and the developer tools so you can check the log file for the error.

Before submitting an app to the app stores, you have to check the log files for debug information, warnings, and errors again. Debug information as well as warnings and errors should not be part of the release version of the app.

Also keep the log files of the backend systems in mind as they log different kinds of information such as requests and responses as well.

> **Important**   Some bugs are visible only in the app's log files. Such bugs may not be shown to the user but could have a huge impact on the functionality of the app.

Be Creative!

Up until this point, this book has presented a systematic approach to mobile testing and its specifics. But everyone who has effectively tested software knows that most of the time, the really nasty bugs don't occur systematically. Bugs come in different shapes, sizes, and situations, and sometimes it's really hard to find them.

After you have tested your mobile app in a systematic way (or before starting with the systematic approach), it is useful to think out of the box. Lean back, step away from all the test cases and systematic approaches, and just try to break it! Test the app for a limited time frame—30 minutes, for example—and try to find some bugs using your own creative approaches.

Be creative with your testing. Try to think of edge cases that are most likely to happen in the real world when lots of people will be using the mobile app in a totally different way from what you and your team expect.

Do crazy things with the app and the device. Rotate or flip the device, use more than one hand to interact with the app, and press buttons as fast as possible.

While doing that, watch out for any unexpected behavior, crashes, freezes, error messages that make no sense, and any other strange things. I suggest that you record this kind of test session because it is very likely that any bugs that occur will be hard to reproduce. Another approach can be pair testing, which involves one person testing the app while another person watches and takes notes about the performed tests.

Checklists, Mnemonics, and Mind Maps

This part of the chapter is all about reminders. Your daily testing business is stressful and there are so many things to remember, do, and explore. You may want to use some models or tools to prevent you from forgetting important aspects of your work. Three very nice approaches you can draw upon are

- Checklists
- Mnemonics
- Mind maps

Checklists

Every new feature that will be developed needs to be tested. Software testers usually define test cases in order to systematically test every new feature and avoid forgetting anything. When the test cases are finished, a software tester usually prioritizes the manual test cases for the test automation to extend the regression test suite and avoid manually testing the new feature over and over again. However, not every feature or test case can be automated because the test may be too complex and will most likely end up causing lots of maintenance work.

But what can you do if such a test or feature is critical for the app or the business? Never executing it again is simply not an option.

To help you avoid forgetting important things, you may find it useful to write a checklist with parts of the app that need to be manually tested again before going live or after a project milestone has been reached.

Checklists can be very generic and high level so that they can be used in several different projects, or they can be really low level with specific steps to test a certain feature.

The mobile testing checklist in Table 4.1 is a generic one that covers lots of important aspects of the mobile app testing process. This list can be used for several different mobile apps.

> **Important**   This list is by no means complete; it is merely an example of what a mobile testing checklist could look like.

This checklist shows some possible generic mobile tests that could be executed on top of your systematic testing approach. It may also be useful to create a release checklist for the whole team so they don't miss anything important to the process. However, checklists can be really specific to cover a very special

Table 4.1 *Generic Mobile Testing Checklist*

No.	Description	Expected Result
1	Test the app against the requirements and acceptance criteria.	The app must pass all the requirements and criteria.
2	Test on different platforms and operating system versions.	The app must work on the defined platforms and operating system versions.
3	Check the app in portrait and landscape modes.	The app must work in landscape and portrait modes. The UI must handle the orientation change.
4	Check the design guidelines for the platforms.	The app must follow the UI guidelines to provide a good user experience.
5	Check the development guidelines for the platforms.	The app must follow the development guidelines to pass the store requirements.
6	Test the app on different screen resolutions and screen densities.	The UI elements of the app must be shown in the correct positions. Elements have to work when touched.
7	Use the app in different networks (LTE, 3G, EDGE, GPRS, Wi-Fi).	The app must work at different network speeds. No crashes, no confusing error messages are allowed.
8	Test how the app handles a network change, such as from LTE to EDGE.	The change in network speed should not affect the app.
9	Use the app in airplane mode.	Proper error messages must be given to the user. The app must have access to locally stored data.
10	Use different network providers to test your app.	The app must work with different network providers and network technologies.
11	While fetching data from the backend service, shut down the device's Internet connection.	The app must show a proper error message.

(Continues)

Table 4.1 *Generic Mobile Testing Checklist (Continued)*

No.	Description	Expected Result
12	Turn the Internet connection on and try reloading the data.	The app must fetch data from the backend system and update the UI.
13	Use device-specific hardware functions such as GPS, NFC, the camera, and other sensors.	The app must work with the hardware features of the phone.
14	Test the shutdown of hardware-specific functions within the app.	Check that GPS, for example, is turned off to avoid consuming too much battery.
15	Check battery usage while the app is running.	The app should not consume too much battery while running.
16	Check battery usage while the app is in standby.	Battery consumption should be low when the app is in standby.
17	Check the app's memory usage.	The app should not consume too much memory.
18	Compare the performance of a released app with the new release candidate.	The performance should improve or stay the same.
19	Test the app in different languages.	All elements must be visible on the screen. The UI must look the same in every language.
20	Check the app permissions.	The app should use only the permissions that are required for the app.
21	Check the local database.	The local database should be encrypted. Only required data should be stored.
22	Check the log files within the IDE.	The log files of the release candidate should not include any debug information, warnings, or errors.
23	Check that the app is signed with the correct and valid certificate.	The app must be signed with the company certificate.

Table 4.1 *Generic Mobile Testing Checklist*

No.	Description	Expected Result
24	Install, delete, and update the app on a real device.	Installing, deleting, and updating the app must work. Deleted apps must be removed completely; no data is allowed to be on the device. Updating the app should not affect the stored data and the current state of the app.
25	Check that the app can handle interrupts such as phone calls, SMS, or any other kind of notifications.	The app must handle the notifications correctly with no error messages or crashes.
26	Test the app while you are on the move, such as in a car, on a train, or in the countryside.	The app must work in different usage scenarios.
27	Track post-release actions.	Check user reactions; gather feedback and crash reports.

part of the app, such as the payment and billing processes, or the different sensors and interfaces.

Important   Be creative with checklists. Create your own checklists that are specific to your app and project.

Mnemonics

SFDPOT, FCCCUTSVIDS, and ISLICEDUPFUN are not typos. They're abbreviations for mnemonics. Mnemonics are learning techniques that aid information retention. When it comes to mobile app testing, each letter stands for a testing approach or technique used for software applications. Mnemonics are used to remember important aspects while testing software applications and are very useful for software testers because they are easy to remember and include powerful ideas and best practices on how to test software.

SFDPOT[26] is a mnemonic from Karen Nicole Johnson that she adapted from James Bach's mnemonic SFDPO[27] (better known as "San Francisco Depot") on mobile testing. Karen included the following points:

- **Structure:** Test what it's made of.
  - Can I download the app?
  - Can I download an update?
- **Function:** Test what it does.
  - Does the app or site perform the tasks or features it was designed to?
  - Does the app or site prevent, block, or not include features not intended on a mobile device?
- **Data:** Test what it does it to.
  - Does the app find time-related data based on the device time?
  - Does the app find locations based on my location (such as movie theaters or hotels)?
- **Platform:** Test what it depends upon.
  - Does the app use location services?
  - Does the app depend on any device settings?
- **Operations:** Test how it's used.
  - Does the app function when I am moving and traveling around?
  - What happens when I switch to Wi-Fi versus 3G?
- **Time:** Test how it's affected by time.
  - What happens if the time zone is switched?
  - What happens when my location is switched?

For each part, Karen wrote some questions to ask while testing a mobile app. Check out the full list of questions in her blog post "Applying the SFDPOT Heuristic to Mobile Testing." Use and adapt them to test your app.

---

26. http://karennicolejohnson.com/2012/05/applying-the-sfdpot-heuristic-to-mobile-testing/
27. www.satisfice.com/articles/sfdpo.shtml

Another mnemonic is FCC CUTS VIDS[28] by Mike Kelly, who noted down his ideas in tours to explore and test applications in several ways:

- **Feature tour**
  - Explore the application and get to know all the control elements and features.

- **Complexity tour**
  - Find the most complex parts of the application.

- **Claims tour**
  - Find all the information about the software that tells you what the product does.

- **Configuration tour**
  - Find all the ways to change the settings of the application.

- **User tour**
  - Imagine how the possible users of the application will use the software and what they expect from it.

- **Testability tour**
  - Find all features within the software that could be tested with the help of tools.

- **Scenario tour**
  - Imagine possible scenarios as to how the software will be used by its users.

- **Variability tour**
  - Try to find ways to change the application.

- **Interoperability tour**
  - Does the software interact with other software?

- **Data tour**
  - Find the data elements of the application.

---

28. http://michaeldkelly.com/blog/2005/9/20/touring-heuristic.html

- **Structure tour**
  - Gather as much information as possible about the application, such as the programming language, APIs, hardware, and so on.

The described tours are an excellent way of finding out possible settings, features, or configurations of the software application. Besides that, the tours cover the user's perspective and are ideal for exploring the application. All of the mentioned tours can easily be adapted to mobile apps.

Another great mobile testing mnemonic is I SLICED UP FUN[29] by Jonathan Kohl, who also adapted his mnemonic from James Bach's SFDPO for use with mobile apps. He covered very specific mobile areas that have to be tested during the development phase:

- **Inputs into the device**
  - Built-in keyboard/keypad
  - Touchscreen gestures and typing
  - Syncing with other devices
- **Store**
  - Submission specifications
  - Development guide
  - User guide for error handling, location services, permissions for user privacy items, accessibility, and so on
- **Location**
  - Geolocation errors
  - Movement, stopping suddenly
  - Connection issues due to interference
- **Interactions/interruptions**
  - Running multiple applications, multitasking
  - Using other applications, then using the application you are testing (e-mail, calendar, texting, note taking, others)
  - Notifications appearing

---

29. www.kohl.ca/articles/ISLICEDUPFUN.pdf

- **Communication**
  - Phone
  - Texting
  - E-mails
- **Ergonomics**
  - Small screens can be hard on the eyes.
  - A small device means there is no ergonomic help from a desk or chair—you often hunch over to interact with it.
  - It's not uncommon to get a sore back, fingers, or eyes when using a device for any length of time.
- **Data**
  - Types of input—see if the app uses special characters, different languages, and so on.
  - Media—see if the app depends on an outside source to play music, videos, or anything else.
  - Size of files—if the application uses outside files, try using different file types.
- **Usability**
  - Note and log any issues that make you uncomfortable, frustrated, angry, or upset while using the app.
- **Platform**
  - Android
  - iOS
  - Windows Phone
  - BlackBerry
- **Function**
  - Can you identify everything that the application does?
  - Have you worked through all the aspects of the app? Clicked every button? Filled in every form?
  - Try a tour of the product to identify everything it does.

- **User scenarios**
  - How is this application supposed to be used?
  - What problems does it solve for users?
  - What are the goals of end users that this application helps them solve?
- **Network**
  - Wi-Fi
  - Wireless broadband
  - Dead spots

I SLICED UP FUN is a very good mnemonic, and mobile testers should know it in order to improve their testing work and to remember the important mobile aspects. Besides his mnemonic, Jonathan wrote an excellent book about mobile testing called *Tap into Mobile Application Testing*,[30] which is available on Leanpub and covers lots of mobile testing topics. The tour chapter is really interesting and an excellent source of knowledge.

The last mnemonic about mobile testing I want to mention is COP FLUNG GUN,[31] created by the company Moolya. This mnemonic covers the following topics and is worth looking at:

- Communication
- Orientation
- Platform
- Function
- Location
- User scenarios
- Notifications
- Guidelines
- Gesture
- Updates
- Network

---

30. https://leanpub.com/testmobileapps
31. http://moolya.com/blogs/2012/04/121/Test-Mobile-applications-with-COP-who-FLUNG-GUN

> **Important**   Mnemonics are great approaches you can use to remind yourself of important things. They will help you organize your testing approach, testing strategy, and thoughts.

Mind Maps

Mind maps are another great way to visually organize information as they can help you to process your thoughts and ideas on certain topics such as mobile testing. Rosie Sherry, the woman behind Ministry of Testing,[32] a platform and professional community for software testers who lead the way in software testing content, training, and events, created and published two great mind maps about mobile testing. One of her mind maps is shown in Figures 4.3 through 4.8.

Both mind maps can be downloaded in high resolution from Ministry of Testing 1[33] and Ministry of Testing 2.[34] The mind maps Rosie created are based on the mnemonic from Karen Nicole Johnson.

Another great interactive mind map project is the Testing Map,[35] which covers lots of different areas of software testing and provides some really useful ideas.

> **Important**   Try to create your own mind map based on your app by adding possible testing tasks. Furthermore, print it out and put it up in the office. That way, your colleagues will stand to benefit from it as well.

How to File Mobile Bugs

We've now come to the last topic in this chapter, "How to File Mobile Bugs." If you find a bug within a mobile app, you need to report it in order to get it fixed. Filing mobile bug reports requires some additional information that the developers need in order to reproduce and fix the bug.

But what is important when filing a mobile bug? What should a bug report look like? Before I answer those two questions, I want to raise another one: Why even send a bug report?

---

32. www.ministryoftesting.com/
33. www.ministryoftesting.com/2012/06/getting-started-with-mobile-testing-a-mindmap/
34. www.ministryoftesting.com/2012/05/mobile-testing-course-pictures-and-a-mindmap/
35. http://thetestingmap.org/

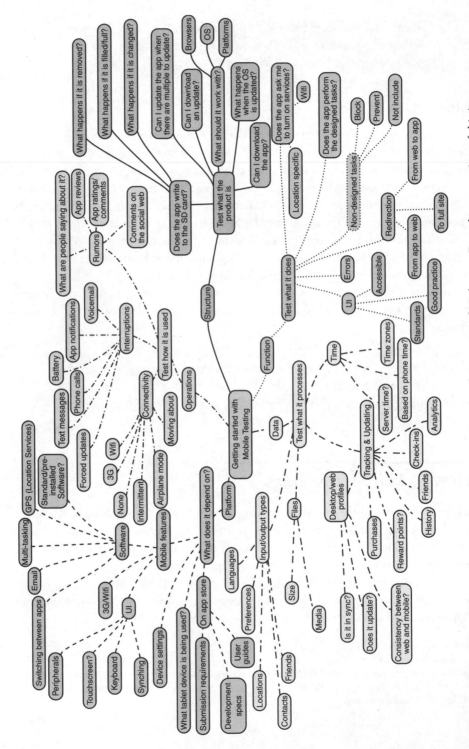

Figure 4.3 *Mobile testing mind map. Courtesy of Rosie Sherry and Karen Nicole Johnson. For a larger version of this image, see* informit.com/title/9780134191713

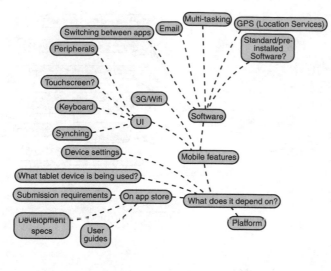

Figure 4.4 *Mobile testing mind map: mobile platforms. Courtesy of Rosie Sherry and Karen Nicole Johnson*

Figure 4.5 *Mobile testing mind map: mobile operations. Courtesy of Rosie Sherry and Karen Nicole Johnson*

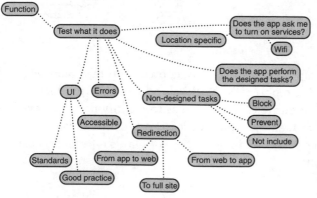
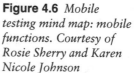

Figure 4.6 *Mobile testing mind map: mobile functions. Courtesy of Rosie Sherry and Karen Nicole Johnson*

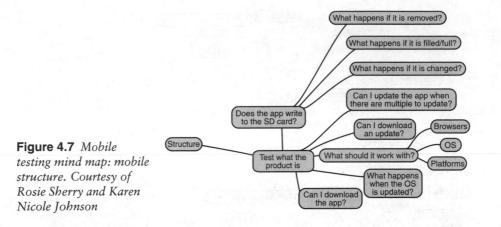

Figure 4.7 *Mobile testing mind map: mobile structure. Courtesy of Rosie Sherry and Karen Nicole Johnson*

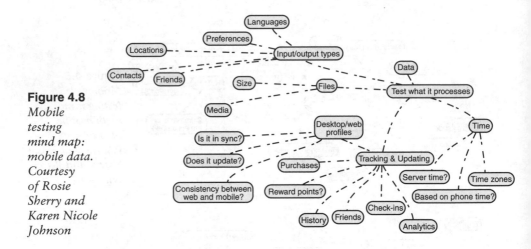

Figure 4.8 *Mobile testing mind map: mobile data. Courtesy of Rosie Sherry and Karen Nicole Johnson*

Bug reports are very important for the product owner, product manager, and the developers. First, a bug report tells the developers and the product owner about issues they were not aware of. It also helps to identify possible new features no one has thought of, and last but not least, it provides useful information about how a customer may use the software. All of this information can be used to improve your software.

Whenever you find something strange, if something behaves differently or looks weird, don't hesitate to file a bug report.

Let's come to the question of what a bug report should look like and what's important when filing it.

A bug report should contain as much information as possible in order to identify, reproduce, and fix the bug. That said, your report should only include information that's important to handling the bug, so try to avoid adding any useless information. Another important point is that you should describe only one error per bug report. Don't combine, group, or create containers for bugs. It's likely that not all of the bugs will be fixed at the same time, so refrain from combining or grouping them.

The information described in the following sections should be included in a bug report.

Bug ID

A bug must have a unique identifier such as a number or a combination of characters and numbers. If you're using a defect management tool, the tool will handle the bug IDs for you. If not, think about a unique ID system for your project.

- **Bad:** *123* is a unique ID, but you might have several projects whose IDs are the same.
- **Good:** *AppXYZ-123* is good because you're combining an ID with a project abbreviation and a number.

Description

Create a short but meaningful description in order to provide the developer with a quick overview of what went wrong without going into detail. You should, for example, include error codes or the part of the application where the bug occurred.

- **Bad:** "The app crashed," "White page," "Saw an error," "Bug"
- **Good:** "Error Code 542 on detail message view" or "Time-out when sending a search request"

Steps to Reproduce

This is one of the most important points. Provide the exact steps together with the input data on how to reproduce the bug. If you are able to provide this kind of information, the bug will be very easy to fix in most cases.

- **Bad:** "I tried to execute a search."
- **Good:** "Start the app and enter 'Mobile Testing' into the search input field. Press the search button and you'll see the error code 783 on the search result page header."

Expected Result

In this section you should describe what you expected to happen when the bug occurred.

- **Bad:** "It should work" or "I didn't expect it to crash."
- **Good:** "I expected to see a search results page with a scrollable list of 20 entries."

Actual Result

What happened when the bug occurred? Write down the actual result, what went wrong, or the error that was returned.

- **Bad:** "It just won't work."
- **Good:** "The search results page was empty" or "I got the error code 567 on the search results page."

Work-around

If you've found a way to continue using the app and avoid the bug, explain your steps. Those steps are important to know since the work-around could cause other problems or indicate a way in which the app should not be used. On the other hand, a work-around can be very useful for the customer support team in order to help customers solve the current problem until the bug gets fixed.

- **Bad:** "I found a work-around."
- **Good:** "If you put the device into landscape mode, the search button is enabled and the user can search again."

Reproducible

If you found a reproducible bug, that's fine, but does it occur every time? If it happens every time, that's great as it should be an easy fix for the developer. But if the bug occurs only 20% of the time, it is much harder to find a solution. Make sure you provide this information, as it is very useful for the developer and will prevent the bug from being closed with the comment "Can't be reproduced."

- **Bad:** "Sometimes"
- **Good:** "The bug occurs two out of ten times."

Operating System, Mobile Platform, and Mobile Device

Another important component of a bug report is information about the operating system, the mobile platform, and the mobile device. Write down the operating system, mobile platform, and device on which the bug occurred.

- **Bad:** "On Android" or "On iOS"
- **Good:** "Android, Version 4.1.2 Google Nexus 4" or "iOS, Version 6.1 iPhone 4S"

Mobile-Device-Specific Information

Mobile devices have lots of interfaces and sensors that could have an impact on your app. The battery could also affect the app you're testing. Write down all of this information in your bug report.

- **Bad:** No information
- **Good:** "GPS sensor activated, changed the orientation from landscape to portrait mode" or "Used the device in a sunny place" or "Battery state was 15%" or "Battery state was 100%."

Browser Version

If your app is a mobile Web app and you found an issue, it's very important to note the browser version where you found the bug as it may occur only in a certain browser version.

- **Bad:** "Google Chrome" or "Mozilla Firefox"
- **Good:** "Google Chrome version 45.35626" or "Mozilla Firefox 27.6"

Software Build Version

Another really useful piece of information is the current build version of the app where the bug occurred. This will prevent the developer from wasting time trying to reproduce a bug that's already been fixed in the current code base.

- **Bad:** No information
- **Good:** "App build version 1.2.3"

Network Condition and Environment

When filing a mobile bug, it's important to provide some information about the network condition and the environment in which the bug occurred. This will help to identify the problem more easily and will possibly show some side effects no one has thought of.

- **Bad:** No information or "Happened on my way to work"
- **Good:** "I was connected to a 3G network while I was walking through the city center."

Language

If your app supports several languages, provide this information in your bug report.

- **Bad:** No information
- **Good:** "I was using the German-language version of the app."

Test Data

A complete bug report must include the test data that was used to reproduce the bug. Simple test data can be login credentials with username and password. However, in some cases it is not enough to provide just a username and password. It is very likely that you need to provide complete test data sets, for example, as an SQL dump or a test data script that will generate the necessary data.

- **Bad:** No information
- **Good:** "Find the attached SQL script to put the database in the defined state" or "Enter 'Mobile Testing' into the search input field."

Severity

Every bug you find needs a severity level. Either your defect management tool will offer you some categories, or you have to define them with your team. It is important to give a bug a severity level as it will allow the team to prioritize their bug-fixing time so that critical and high-priority bugs will be fixed first. If this information is not provided, it takes much more time to find the bugs that need to be fixed before the release. The default severities are Critical, High, Medium, and Low.

- **Bad:** No information
- **Good:** "Critical" or "Medium"

Bug Category

In addition to the severity level, the bug category is also a very useful piece of information. The product owner or the developer can filter by category to get an overview of the current status of bugs per category. For example, if there are lots of UX bugs, this may be an indicator of a poor UI and UX or a missing design expert in the team, meaning that the app needs some more design improvements.

- **Bad:** "No information"
- **Good:** "Functionality" or "UX" or "Performance"

Screenshot or Video

Whenever you find a bug, try to create screenshots or a video to provide the developer with more information. When providing a screenshot, use an image-editing tool to mark the bug in the screenshot. A video is also a great way to describe a bug you've come across. It is also very useful to give the screenshot or the video a good name or description.

- **Bad:** "No screenshots or videos attached" or "Screenshot1.png"
- **Good:** "01_InsertSearchTerm.png, 02_SearchResultPageWithError.png"

Log Files

If your app crashes or freezes, connect the device to your computer and read out the log files. In most cases a stack trace will be shown with a description of the error. This kind of information is extremely useful for developers, as they know right away in which class the bug or the error has occurred.

- **Bad:** "No information provided when the app crashed."
- **Good:** "Provided the full stack trace in the bug report" or "Attached the log file to the report."

Tester Who Found the Bug

Write down your name or the name of the tester who found the bug. Developers or product owners may have some questions about the reported bug, and they will of course want to get in touch directly with the tester who found it. In most cases, this is automatically done by the defect management system where each user has his or her own account. If not, make sure you add your e-mail address and/or phone number.

- **Bad:** No information
- **Good:** "Daniel Knott, daniel@adventuresinqa.com"

Three More Points

As you have seen, there is a lot of information that should be included in a bug report. There are three other points you should keep in mind when writing a bug report.

The first one is *Don't get personal*. When filing a bug report, describe the software misbehavior rather than the developer's mindset or the quality of his or her work. Don't use offensive or emotionally charged words as those kinds of reports will be ignored by the developer and will end up causing bad blood within the team.

The second one is *It's not you*. It's not your fault that the bug occurred. It is the software that's broken, and you and your colleagues need to fix it.

And the third point is *Keep it simple*. Try to write your bug report in such a way that someone with no idea about the project or the app is able to understand the problem. If the bug report is that easy, every developer within the team will be able to fix it and nontechnical colleagues can understand the problem and will value your work.

App Quality Alliance

If you want to get further information about how to test your Android or iOS app, have a look at the nonprofit group App Quality Alliance site.[36] This group is headed by different core members and knowledge contributors such as AT&T, LGE, Microsoft, Motorola, Oracle, Samsung, and Sony Mobile. The main aim of the group is to work very closely with the industry to improve the quality of mobile apps.

The group devised testing criteria for Android and iOS apps. You can download both PDF documents via the following links:

- Testing criteria for Android apps (www.appqualityalliance.org/AQuA-test-criteria-for-android-apps)

- Testing criteria for iOS apps (www.appqualityalliance.org/AQuA-test-criteria-for-iOS-apps)

Both documents contain lots of test cases that your app should run through before you submit it to the app stores.

The group also provides information about mobile app performance testing as well as best-practice guidelines for developing quality mobile apps. You can download both documents via the following links:

- Performance testing criteria (www.appqualityalliance.org/aqua-performance-test-criteria)

- Best-practice guidelines for developing quality mobile apps (www.appqualityalliance.org/AQuA-best-practice-guidelines)

The group's Web site is definitely worth checking out, and maybe you'd even like to contribute.

Summary

Chapter 4 is one of the main chapters of this book and contains lots of testing ideas and solutions that can be used in your daily working life. The chapter started with a description of the differences among emulators, simulators, and

---

36. www.appqualityalliance.org/

real devices and what is important to know about them. Before the hands-on part of the chapter I explained the difference between manual and automated testing as well as the role of traditional testing in the mobile testing business. If you are familiar with "traditional" software testing such as for Web or desktop applications, that knowledge is also useful for mobile apps. Lots of the testing approaches for Web or desktop applications are also valid for mobile apps such as white box and black box testing techniques. However, when it comes to mobile testing, there are more areas you need to test in order to be sure that your app is working on different levels and with different hardware and software versions. In this chapter I described the following mobile-related topics:

- Mobile usability testing
- Accessibility testing
- Battery usage testing
- Stress and interrupt testing
- Performance testing
- Standby testing
- Installation testing
- Update testing
- Database testing
- Local storage testing
- Security testing
- Platform guideline testing
- Conformance testing
- Checking the log files

I also provided checklists of sample test cases that can be executed, such as before the app is submitted to an app store. Furthermore, I showed different mnemonics and mind maps that can be useful for your mobile testing activities.

The chapter ended with a detailed overview of how to file a mobile bug with lots of do's and don'ts.

Chapter 5

Mobile Test Automation and Tools

This chapter is all about tools. I describe the different types and concepts of mobile test automation tools and give you some advice on where to automate and how to select a mobile test automation tool for your app and development environment. I also explain continuous integration and beta distribution tools.

This chapter doesn't cover how to install and configure the different mobile test automation tools. The reason for this is simple: The tools provide installation and configuration guides already, so you can just visit their Web sites to find all the information you need. Details about each tool will be provided in the relevant sections of this chapter.

The Flipped Testing Pyramid

Before I start with the mobile test automation tools, I want to briefly explain the test automation pyramid. Anyone who is involved in software testing and software test automation should know the test automation pyramid introduced by Mike Cohn.[1]

As you can see in Figure 5.1, the typical pyramid consists of three layers. At the bottom there is the automated unit testing layer; in the middle, the automated integration testing layer; and at the top, there is the automated end-to-end (E2E) testing layer (including the user interface tests). Each layer has a different size, indicating the number of tests that should be written within each

---

1. www.mountaingoatsoftware.com/

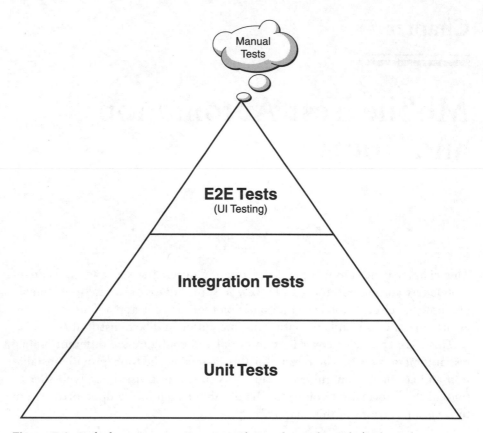

Figure 5.1 *Default test automation pyramid. Based on a figure by Mike Cohn.*

stage. Manual testing is not part of the test pyramid; hence it is shown as a cloud for additional testing work.

But this pyramid is not applicable to mobile apps and mobile test automation. As you learned several chapters ago, mobile testing requires a totally different set of tests—movement, sensors, different devices and networks—from other software such as desktop or Web applications. Lots of manual testing is required to be sure that a mobile app is working as expected in the different usage scenarios.

Mobile test automation tools are not currently as mature as their counterparts for Web and desktop applications, which leads to a flipped test automation pyramid. As the tools become increasingly mature, this pyramid is likely to flip back again because the default test automation pyramid is based on a more stable foundation (see Figure 5.1). The default pyramid therefore can't be used as an indicator of test automation and manual testing in the mobile world.

The flipped testing pyramid looks like Figure 5.2.

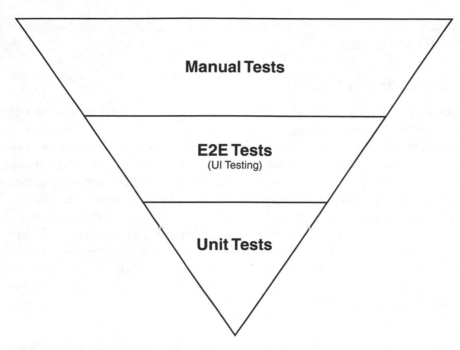

Figure 5.2 *The flipped testing pyramid*

In this version of the pyramid, the automated unit testing layer is the smallest one. This is the case because not every unit or method of mobile apps can be tested in an isolated manner. In some cases, different APIs, layers, or systems may need to be faked or mocked in order to get the small unit to work. This is also the case for every other software application, but in some cases mocking or faking other systems for mobile apps is much more complex. This is not efficient from a technical or economic point of view. However, it's no excuse for not writing mobile unit tests at all. The business logic of an app must be tested at the unit level.

The next stage is the end-to-end test automation layer. Within this layer, the app is tested from a user perspective to make sure the whole system is working, from the app's user interface through to the backend system via a wireless network, including integration testing with different libraries or APIs. The integration testing layer is therefore part of the end-to-end layer.

The biggest change in this pyramid is that manual testing is part of it. Mobile testing requires lots of manual testing, and this can't yet be replaced by test automation or any other tools.

Nevertheless, mobile test automation is a really important topic, and every mobile tester should be able to write automated regression tests that provide fast feedback about the current quality state of an app. Furthermore, test automation helps the team build a reliable and robust mobile app that makes the customers happy.

The Mobile Test Pyramid

The flipped testing pyramid has no stable foundation, and mobile testing requires lots of manual testing, which is why I created my own mobile test pyramid consisting of four layers including manual and automated steps (see Figure 5.3). The biggest layer of the pyramid, manual testing, forms the strong foundation for every mobile app project, followed by end-to-end testing, beta testing, and a top layer comprising unit testing. The gray parts of the pyramid indicate the automated steps, and the white parts are the manual testing steps. The beta testing layer is new to the pyramid but essential to every mobile app project. Keeping the high expectations of mobile users in mind requires that this layer be part of every mobile project to get early feedback from your mobile customers. You can either use a crowd testing approach for your beta testing, or you can ask your colleagues to beta-test early versions of your app to provide important feedback.

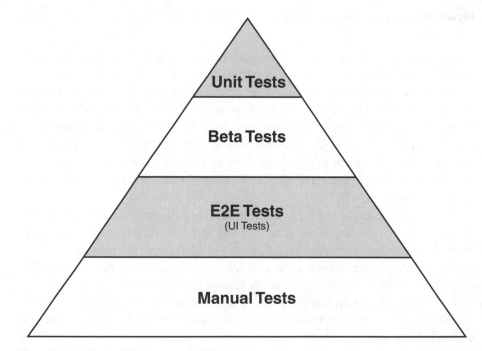

Figure 5.3 *The mobile test pyramid*

I have used this mobile test pyramid in several projects and it helped me set up a reliable, effective, and valuable testing process.

> **Important**   Keep the problem of the flipped pyramid in mind and use the mobile test pyramid in your project to have a good mix of manual and automated testing.

In this chapter, I focus more on the end-to-end test automation tools because those are the tools mobile testers will most likely work with. However, some unit testing tools are also mentioned.

Different Types of Test Automation Tools

Before you start with mobile test automation, it is important that you understand the underlying architecture of the different mobile platforms. You need to know how to access the different objects of app-like buttons, labels, lists, views, and any other kind of element in order to interact with those elements during the test run.

You also need to be able to write code and build up reliable test automation suites that are integrated within your app's development pipeline.

When selecting a tool, you should know the different types and concepts of mobile test automation tools and how those tools access the different objects. This is important to know when selecting a tool for your needs and project because each approach has its pros and cons.

Image Recognition

Tools that use the image recognition approach compare images in order to drive the user interface of an app. When writing the test automation script, you take screenshots, for example, of buttons or labels that are embedded into your script. When the script is executed, the image recognition tool compares the current screen with the stored baseline image. If the stored image is found on the screen, the script will execute the programmed steps.

Those kinds of tools are really useful if the UI of the app doesn't change too often, is developed for several mobile platforms, and has exactly the same user interface and control elements. In that case, image recognition tools are a great and fast way of writing test automation for cross-platform mobile apps.

The biggest disadvantage of image recognition tools is the high maintenance involved with the test scripts. The scripts will not work if the orientation of the device is changed, such as from portrait to landscape mode, on bigger screens, or if the screen resolution changes. Another drawback is testing an app in different languages, which is not possible since the captured images are available only in one language and will not work with other languages.

Here are some examples of image recognition tools:

- eggPlant (www.testplant.com/eggplant/testing-tools/eggplant-mobile-eggon/)
- RoutineBot (www.routinebot.com/)
- Sikuli (www.sikuli.org/)
- TestObject (https://testobject.com/)

Coordinate-Based Recognition

Coordinate-based recognition tools rely on predefined x and y axis coordinates to access and interact with the UI elements of the app. If the coordinates of the element change, the whole script needs to be adapted to the new values. This has a major impact on the maintenance of the scripts in order to build reliable tests.

Here are some examples of coordinate-based recognition tools:

- MonkeyTalk (www.cloudmonkeymobile.com/monkeytalk)
- Perfecto Mobile (www.perfectomobile.com/)

OCR/Text Recognition

Mobile test automation tools that use the OCR and text recognition approach obtain the text of the control elements that are visible on the screen of the mobile device. To determine if the text is visible on the screen, OCR technology is used.

OCR and text recognition tools can handle different screen resolutions, orientations, and sizes. However, such tools can verify only text elements that are visible on the screen. If the text changes or is removed from the app, the UI element is very difficult (or impossible) to identify. You are not able to check if, for example, a UI view is visible, if a list is present, or if elements without text are shown on the screen. Another drawback of OCR recognition tools is that they are very slow because the whole screen needs to be scanned for the text.

Here are some examples of OCR/text recognition tools:

- eggPlant
  (www.testplant.com/eggplant/testing-tools/eggplant-mobile-eggon/)
- MonkeyTalk (www.cloudmonkeymobile.com/monkeytalk)
- Robotium (https://code.google.com/p/robotium/)
- SeeTest (http://experitest.com/)
- TestObject (https://testobject.com/)

Native Object Recognition

Tools that use the native object recognition approach detect the UI objects with a UI element tree. The UI elements can be accessed using XPath (XML Path Language), CSS (Cascading Style Sheet) locators, or the native object ID of the element. The native object recognition approach is very common in the different test automation tools covering native, hybrid, and mobile Web apps. This approach enables you to get access to the native elements such as buttons, labels, views, lists, and other kinds of UI elements. If the IDs or the locators are well defined and written, the test scripts are reliable in the event of changes and therefore reusable on other devices as well. This is a huge advantage compared to all of the other tools because the scripts do not depend on changes to the UI, resolution, orientation, or the device itself. The majority of the test automation tools support this approach for detecting the elements.

Here are some examples of native object recognition tools:

- Appium (http://appium.io/)
- Calabash (http://calaba.sh/)
- Espresso (https://code.google.com/p/android-test-kit/)
- Robotium (https://code.google.com/p/robotium/)
- Selendroid (http://selendroid.io/)
- Selenium (http://docs.seleniumhq.org/)
- TenKod EZ TestApp (www.tenkod.com/ez-testapp/)

Capture and Replay

Lots of tool manufacturers advertise capture and replay functionality. Tools that support this technology are able to record actions such as clicking, scrolling, swiping, or typing into a script. With the help of the replay function, the software will execute the exact same actions over and over again. This technology sounds great in theory, but in reality and day-to-day test automation work, capture and replay tools should be used and handled with care. But why?

I have worked with different capture and replay tools, and every tool presented the same problems. The captured scripts were not reliable at all. They were affected by UI, orientation, and screen resolution changes (most of them use coordinate-based or image-based recognition). The scripts were not reusable from device to device or on different mobile operating system versions of the same mobile platform.

Often the scripts were not able to start because the device was not in a defined state, meaning that the tool was not able to replay the script. Often the scripts must be edited manually to be more stable and reliable. Another problem that always occurred was a timing issue as the tools were either too fast or too slow to interact with the application while the script was replayed. The only way to solve this issue was to add wait operations, but this is not a good approach for writing test automation scripts. Using wait or sleep operations is flawed and leads to unreliable test results.

However, there are also some good qualities; for example, mobile testers who have no programming skills can use the tools to generate some basic test automation scripts with very little training. On the other hand, they are not able to modify the script afterward.

However, don't use capture and replay tools to build up a huge test automation suite for your mobile app; otherwise you will end up with a nonmaintainable test suite. I recommend that you use these kinds of tools as a starting point to record basic interactions within your app and get the UI selectors of the elements. The recorded UI selectors or IDs can then be used as a foundation for further programming to build up a test automation suite based on your own programming.

Tool Type Recommendation

Before I recommend a tool type and approach, I want to briefly summarize the mobile test automation tool landscape. Most of the tools are specific to a mobile platform, irrespective of whether they use the image, coordinate, OCR, or native object recognition approach. There are very few tools that support more than one mobile platform such as Android, iOS, Windows Phone, or BlackBerry. However, no tool is able to automate multiple mobile platforms with one test code base. There are some test automation tool providers who promise to be able to automate everything on every mobile platform, but that's not true. Every mobile platform has specific requirements for usability or navigation usage of an app, meaning that you also need to have multiple test code bases in order to automate them.

In most mobile projects, you have to deal with multiple code bases of different programming languages and test automation tools in order to build up a testing and development pipeline.

In my opinion, a mobile test automation tool must be able to access the native object properties that are used to identify and to interact with the native elements. This is the best and most efficient way to write test automation scripts for mobile apps. Writing such test scripts requires more effort and programming skills, but the scripts are much more reliable and robust to changes and can be executed on different devices and screen resolutions.

You should therefore use native object recognition tools in your project based on the app type you are testing (native, hybrid, or Web apps).

> **Important** Remember that some mobile test automation tools support more than one recognition approach. Combine the approaches in your test scripts, but keep the pros and cons in mind as well as the fact that no tool is perfect.

What Should Be Automated?

When you have the task of determining which tests should be automated or not, keep one thing in mind: It is impossible to automate every feature or test case of a mobile app.

Now, you have to answer this question: What should be automated?

Creating a smart mobile test automation plan requires careful planning and design work that should be performed before automating a single test case. First, you should define a goal for your mobile test automation and determine what kinds of tests you want to automate. Keeping the mobile test pyramid in mind can help you to define the unit tests and end-to-end user tests. But you should still remember that you need lots of manual mobile testing and that not everything can be automated. However, you can turn some manual tests into automated tests to save time and testing effort.

Possible goals for your mobile test automation could be:

- Automate the business-critical parts.
- Automate user workflows and scenarios.
- Automate only complex app scenarios.
- Automate sequences that need to be repeated several times.

- Automate only the acceptance criteria.
- Build up a regression test suite.
- Automate only if it is economically reasonable.

If some test cases are performed only a few times, it's probably more economical to leave them for manual testing. If you're worried about forgetting them, add them to a checklist. Tests that need to be run frequently and require lots of inputs and actions should be automated. But don't create large and complex automated test scenarios as those kinds of tests are difficult to maintain, edit, and debug and are likely not to be stable. Keep the tests small and independent of one another.

It is also important to keep the critical parts of the app in mind such as the login or payment process as they have a huge impact on the app, your business, and the people who use it. If the critical parts are not well tested or automated, you may suffer a lot of damage to your reputation.

Another important factor when deciding which tests are to be automated is the time and the money involved. If you need lots of time to automate a mobile test scenario, ask yourself if it is worth automating as a lot of time spent on one specific scenario will cost lots of money. And is the invested time saved later on when the test is automated rather than manual? Ask yourself this question from time to time; you may find that it's OK to test manually.

When automating a test for a mobile app, keep the different mobile devices in mind. Only automate the tests that can be executed on every target device. Try to automate the tests in as general a manner as possible so you can execute them on several devices. And don't forget to automate with different languages if your app is going to be available in various countries. Use the UI element IDs to identify and drive those elements and to implement robust tests.

There is no generic answer to the question "What should be automated?" The answer will be different for every mobile app and depend on the app type, mobile platform, and app purpose.

Every mobile tester should keep the following points in mind when answering this question:

- It is not possible to automate testing of the entire app or all of its features.
- Define a goal for your test automation.
- Define end-to-end tests.
- Start test automation as early as possible together with the app development.
- Keep the time and the costs that are needed for the test automation in mind.

- Keep the tests small, fast, simple, and independent.
- Keep the different mobile devices in mind.
- Execute the tests as early as possible and as often as possible.

> **Important**   Don't try to automate everything. Define test automation goals depending on your app and start automating those goals.

Emulator, Simulator, or Real Device?

The next question you need to answer is whether you should automate with emulators, simulators, or real devices. In Chapter 4, "How to Test Mobile Apps," I described the differences among emulators, simulators, and real devices when mobile testing is performed manually. My recommendation there was to use the emulators/simulators for very basic tests and to do manual testing on real devices. But is this also the case with mobile test automation?

Before I answer this question, let's have a look at the pros and cons of emulators/simulators and real devices.

Emulator/Simulator Pros

The biggest advantage of emulators/simulators is the price. Both are free to use and are part of the SDK from the different mobile platforms. Besides that, they are really simple to use and offer various options for developers and testers. After the emulator/simulator is installed, you can create the simulators/emulators using different configurations such as operating system versions or screen resolutions.

Emulator/Simulator Cons

If we look at the cons of the emulators/simulators, there are some more points that you should be aware of. Using emulators/simulators increases the risk of missing important bugs that occur only on real devices. Emulators/simulators are not the same as the real environment, which is a huge disadvantage. Additionally, emulators/simulators offer only a "plain" and simple mobile operating system. They offer no diversity in terms of the different devices, operating systems, and adaptations of the user interface. This is especially the case with Android where several device manufacturers change the UI of the Android system to suit their needs. From a hardware perspective, they also fail to offer a real device environment with all of the relevant sensors and interfaces.

The next disadvantage of mobile emulators/simulators is that the data networks are not real. Network speeds can be simulated, but this will not cover the real data networks with traffic loss or change in network speeds and technologies. And, finally, emulators/simulators do not offer the same performance as real devices in terms of CPU, GPU, memory, or sensors.

Every mobile tester should keep the following points in mind when using emulators or simulators within a project:

- It is risky not to test in a real environment.
- There is no diversity in terms of hardware and software.
- The network environment is simulated.
- There is no real device performance.
- There is no access to device-specific hardware elements such as the camera, GPS, or other sensors.

Real Device Pros

Testing on real devices offers lots of advantages compared to an emulator/simulator. The tests will be executed in a real user environment and therefore the results will be closer to a real user experience, including any discovered bugs. Testing on real devices also offers the option of using the full device's hardware, software, and device-specific features such as sensors, CPU, GPU, and memory. Using the real device for testing shows the real behavior in terms of performance.

The following points summarize the pros of using real devices for testing:

- Real device testing offers reliable test results.
- Real hardware and software features are used.
- The real user experience and app performance can be tested.
- Tests are done in real data networks.

Real Device Cons

Testing on real devices also has some disadvantages. The biggest one is the cost of buying all of the different mobile devices for developing and testing purposes. If you want to test on real devices, you have to buy new devices nearly every month in order to verify that your app runs on all the new features (hardware and software). In addition, you need someone who is responsible for maintaining all those devices. It's not enough just to buy them; you need to come up with a strategy for how to update the devices to newer versions and how to use them within your company.

The following points summarize the cons of using real devices for testing:

- The cost of having to frequently buy new devices is high.
- Maintenance of all the devices is time-consuming.

Where to Automate?

If we look at all the pros and cons, I think the answer to the question "Where to automate?" is pretty simple: on the real device!

Very simple and basic functional tests and test automation can of course be performed on an emulator/simulator to get fast feedback about the current state of a mobile app, and this is especially useful for developers.

However, if you as a mobile tester want to be sure that your app is using all the device-specific elements such as the hardware and software resources during the test automation session, you need to execute the tests on real devices. Executing the test automation scripts on real devices provides you with much better results in terms of reliability, performance, and real-world behavior of the app. Furthermore, you are able to execute the tests on several devices at the same time to quickly determine whether or not an app has a problem on a certain mobile device.

A good approach is to find a healthy mix of emulators, simulators, and real devices to get the best out of your test automation. It is enough if, for example, developers do their test automation on emulators and simulators because scaling and executing test automation scripts in parallel on emulators/simulators is much easier and cheaper than on real devices. If you want to scale and build up an emulator/simulator matrix for your test automation, have a look at the Google TechTalk "Breaking the Matrix—Android Testing at Scale."[2]

You as a mobile tester should write test automation scripts that will run on real devices as well as simulators/emulators.

> **Important**   When selecting a mobile test automation tool, verify that the tool is able to execute the tests on both real devices and emulators/simulators.

---

2. www.youtube.com/watch?v=uHoB0KzQGRg

How to Select the Right Mobile Test Automation Tool

So far you have learned about the different types of test automation tools as well as what should be automated and where the test automation should be performed. Now it is time to find the right mobile test automation tool for your app and your test and development environment.

When selecting a mobile test automation tool, you should keep some points in mind. The first point is that there is no "one size fits all" test automation tool available on the market. Every tool has its pros and cons, and not every tool is suited to every development environment and pipeline. Tool A could work well with project A but not with project B, meaning that the evaluation has to be repeated for every project.

To save some time in the tool evaluation phase, it is a good approach to implement a sample app that includes all of the elements your production app will have in order to see if the test automation tool is able to handle and interact with them. If the tool is able to fulfill all of your requirements for the sample app, you have probably found the right mobile test automation tool for your project.

The second point you should keep in mind is that mobile test automation requires programming skills in order to build up a robust, maintainable, and stable test automation suite. Do not use a capture and replay tool to compensate for a lack of programming skills; you will end up with a real nightmare scenario because you can't fix the broken scripts. If you have no programming skills, try to learn them as you will need them in the future.

Besides developing a sample app to evaluate the mobile test automation tool, you can use the checklist in the next section with some selection criteria. This list will help you to find the tool best suited to your development and testing process.

Selection Criteria for a Test Automation Tool

The following points should be considered when selecting a mobile test automation tool:

1. Does the tool support different mobile app types (native, hybrid, Web apps)?

2. Which mobile platforms are supported (Android, iOS, Windows Phone, BlackBerry)?

3. Which recognition technology does the tool use (native, image, text, coordinate)?

4. Does the tool change the app you want to test (for example, by adding a server, instrumentation)?

5. Is the tool able to execute the tests on real devices as well as on emulators and simulators?

6. Is there a report available at the end of the test run?

7. Is the tool able to take screenshots while the tests are executed, and are those screenshots part of the test report?

8. Can the test suite be executed on several devices at the same time?

9. How long is the test execution time? Is it sufficient for your needs?

10. Does the tool support all of the UI and control elements of the mobile platform?

11. Is there support for a change of orientation from portrait to landscape and vice versa?

12. Is the tool able to awake the device from the sleep or standby mode?

13. Are all gestures supported, such as swipe, scroll, click, tap, or pinch to zoom?

14. Is the tool able to simulate native buttons such as the back or home button?

15. Does the tool use the device's soft keyboard to enter data?

16. Can the app be tested in several languages?

17. Does the tool require modification to match the real device (jailbreak, rooting)?

18. Does the tool support a programming language with which you are able to write test scripts?

19. Is the tool able to execute the tests from the command line?

20. Can the tool be integrated into your development environment (IDE)?

21. Can the tool be integrated into a continuous integration system?

22. Can the tool be combined with other tools such as a defect management or test management tool?

23. Is the tool able to connect to a test cloud provider in order to execute the tests within a cloud?

24. Is the tool well documented?

25. Is the tool open source or closed source?

26. Is there a large community/support behind the tool?

27. Since when has the tool been available on the market and is it used by other companies for mobile test automation?

28. Does the tool support cross-platform tests?

As you can see from the criteria list, there are lots of things to consider when selecting a mobile test automation tool. The evaluation phase is very important and should not be underestimated. If you choose the wrong tool (due to time constraints, for example) before the project starts, it is very likely that you will struggle with the tool during the project.

Point 18 in the list, "Does the tool support a programming language with which you are able to write test scripts?" is very important. You should try to find a tool that supports the programming language with which you are able to write code; this will reduce your learning curve because you need to become familiar with just the tool and not the programming language. You'll also save lots of time and money on additional training.

> **Important**   Develop a sample app or use a checklist with your criteria to find the tool that best fits your test and development process.

Current State of Tools

This part of the chapter should give you an overview of possible mobile test automation tools. I selected mainly open-source end-to-end testing tools for the iOS and Android mobile platforms and tools that I have used in mobile projects. Furthermore, I chose tools that are well known for mobile test automation and used by most companies. I will give you some recommendations and useful information about the tools and how to use them. I will not explain or describe the installation or configuration process of the tools because this information can (or will) be outdated soon. All of the mentioned tools require programming skills in order for you to be able to work with them efficiently.

And, as always, the list of tools mentioned here is by no means complete.

Android Tools

Most of the Android test automation tools are based on the Android Instrumentation Framework[3] from Google. To get started with Android test automation, you need to understand the view hierarchy of an Android app. You also

---

3. http://developer.android.com/tools/testing/testing_android.html

need to know what kinds of components and elements the app uses as well as how all these elements are arranged on the screen and what they represent in the logical structure of the app.

Google provides a very useful tool called UI Automator Viewer[4] to inspect the app's view and layout hierarchy. This tool lets you view the properties—the name or ID of each UI component that is displayed on the screen. You need this kind of information (name or ID of an element) to write your mobile test scripts.

You can find the UI Automator Viewer in the Android SDK location on your computer, for example:

```
/android/sdk/tools/uiautomatorviewer.sh
```

This tool is particularly important when the Android app code is not available and you just have the compiled .apk file to write your mobile test automation. However, some of the Android tools mentioned offer their own UI automator viewer that can be used to inspect the elements.

Robotium

Robotium[5] is the de facto standard open-source tool for Android test automation and was one of the first Android test automation tools on the market. Robotium is a black box tool that provides full support for native and hybrid Android apps. Robotium is an extension of the aforementioned Android Instrumentation Framework and provides a very simple and basic API for writing UI tests. It supplies the so-called `solo` object to call methods such as `clickOnText` or `enterText`. Check out the code in Listing 5.1 for some possible test actions.

Listing 5.1 *Sample Code from Robotium*

```
/* Robotium will click on the text "Welcome" */
solo.clickOnText("Welcome");
/* Robotium will enter the string MySecretPassword into the input
field with the ID 2 */
solo.enterText(2, "MySecretPassword");
/* Robotium will click on the button with the label "Login" */
solo.clickOnButton("Login");
/* Robotium will simulate a click on the native back button */
solo.goBack();
```

4. http://developer.android.com/tools/testing/testing_ui.html
5. https://code.google.com/p/robotium/

Robotium requires only minimal knowledge of the app you want to test and provides excellent readability. By just reading the test methods you already know what is happening and what will be tested on the view of the device. The UI Automator Viewer supplies all of the view information you need to write your tests. Robotium tests are written in the Java programming language and can be executed on a real device or on emulators. Tests can be executed on only a single device at a time, and Robotium is able to test only the app that is being tested, meaning that there is no way of testing outside this application. At the end of the test run a JUnit report is generated.

The written tests can be executed either from the command line, from an IDE, or from a continuous integration server using Maven, Gradle, or Ant.

If you want to know more about Robotium and how to get started, check out the Robotium wiki page:

- Robotium Getting Started
  (https://code.google.com/p/robotium/wiki/Getting_Started)

Also check out the Robotium project pages:

- Latest Robotium version and samples
  (https://code.google.com/p/robotium/wiki/Downloads)

Robotium Extensions

In 2014, the developer of Robotium, Renas Reda, founded the company Robotium[6] to provide the so-called Robotium Recorder, which allows developers and testers to record Robotium tests instead of writing the code manually.

Another nice extension for Robotium is the ExtSolo[7] project from the company Bitbar. ExtSolo adds some very useful test methods to Robotium such as the following:

- `changeDeviceLanguage(java.util.Locale locale)`: switches the current language of the device during the test execution
- `setGPSMockLocation(double latitude, double longitude, double altitude)`: sets the device's current GPS location
- `turnWifi(boolean enabled)`: turns Wi-Fi off and on, to see how the app handles the connection loss

---

6. http://robotium.com/
7. http://docs.testdroid.com/_pages/extsolo.html

Full API documentation is available here:

- ExtSolo API documentation
  (http://docs.testdroid.com/_static/extSolodocs/com/bitbar/recorder/extensions/ExtSolo.html)

Spoon

Spoon[8] is another powerful Android test automation framework, developed by the company Square.[9] Spoon is also an extension of the existing Android Instrumentation Framework. The main difference from Robotium is Spoon's ability to simultaneously execute the same tests on multiple devices or emulators. Spoon can execute the tests on every target (device or emulator) that is visible to adb (Android Debug Bridge) and is connected to the test server.

The tests are also written in Java and can be executed from the command line, from an IDE, or from a continuous integration server. Spoon's structure and test code are also very simple, as you can see in the code in Listing 5.2.

Listing 5.2 *Sample Code from Spoon*

```
Spoon.screenshot(activity, "Login_Screen");
assertThat(password).hasNoError();
instrumentation.runOnMainSync(new Runnable() {
    @Override public void run() {
                password.setText("MySecretPassword");
    }
});
```

After all of these tests have been executed on every device, Spoon generates a static HTML report with detailed information about each device and test (see Figure 5.4). The report compares the test results on the different devices in a nice overview. If screenshots are taken during the test run, Spoon generates an animated GIF image from them so you can see the executed test steps again in the test report.

Spoon also requires very little knowledge of the code for the app you want to test. Spoon can be combined with other Android test automation tools, so you can, for example, use the screenshot function from Spoon and test methods from Robotium or Espresso.

---

8. http://square.github.io/spoon/
9. https://squareup.com

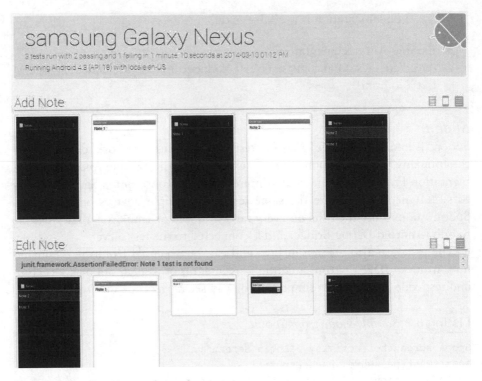

Figure 5.4   *Spoon sample report*

The latest version of Spoon and an example test app can be found on GitHub:

- Spoon samples and latest version (https://github.com/square/spoon)

Selendroid

Selendroid[10] is a test automation tool for native Android, hybrid, or mobile Web apps. The name Selendroid comes from the words **Selen**ium and An**droid**. Selendroid is fully compatible with the JSON Wire Protocol,[11] and the tests are written using the Selenium 2 Client API.[12]

If you are familiar with writing automated tests with Selenium 2 for browser-based applications, it is very easy to write test automation code with Selendroid for Android apps. Selendroid is able to simultaneously execute and interact with multiple Android devices (real devices or emulators).

Listing 5.3 shows a code example.

---

10. http://selendroid.io/
11. https://code.google.com/p/selenium/wiki/JsonWireProtocol
12. http://docs.seleniumhq.org/docs/03_webdriver.jsp

Listing 5.3 *Sample Code from Selendroid*

```
WebElement loginButton = driver().findElement(By.id("startLogin"));
WebElement passwordInput = driver().findElement(By.id("password"));
passwordInput.sendKeys("MySecretPassword");
loginButton.click();
```

The UI elements of the mobile app can be found by different locator types, for example, by ID, name, link text, class, tag name, or XPath. To inspect the UI components of the app under test, Selendroid provides a very useful tool called Selendroid Inspector,[13] which provides a hierarchy viewer that lets you see the UI component properties. It is able to create a screenshot with the view locator, record the click actions on the mobile app, display the HTML source of a Web view, and provide a very useful XPath helper to identify the Web elements.

In order to support different gestures, Selendroid uses the Advanced User Interactions API.[14] The written tests can be executed from the command line, from an IDE, or from a continuous integration server.

Selendroid can be fully integrated as a node into a Selenium Grid[15] for scaling and parallel testing. And, finally, the app under test will not be modified for automation purposes.

Additional useful information on Selendroid can be found on the Web site:

- Selendroid getting started (http://selendroid.io/setup.html)
- Scaling Selendroid (http://selendroid.io/scale.html)
- Latest Selendroid version and samples (https://github.com/selendroid/selendroid)

Calabash for Android

Calabash[16] is a cross-platform mobile test automation framework for native and hybrid Android and iOS apps. The tool makes it possible to write automated UI acceptance tests in Cucumber.[17] With the help of Cucumber, you can express the behavior of the app you're testing using a natural language. This approach is called behavior-driven development (BDD), and it can be very helpful when business experts or nontechnical colleagues are involved in the acceptance criteria process.

---

13. http://selendroid.io/inspector.html
14. https://code.google.com/p/selenium/wiki/AdvancedUserInteractions
15. https://code.google.com/p/selenium/wiki/Grid2
16. http://calaba.sh/
17. http://cukes.info/

Cucumber uses Gherkin[18] as the domain-specific language (DSL) to annotate the behavior of the application.

Please refer to the code in Listings 5.4 and 5.5 for examples. Listing 5.4 shows a Cucumber (Gherkin) scenario using real text to describe the behavior of the application.

Listing 5.4 *Sample Gherkin Code*

```
Feature: As a user I want to login
  Scenario: Login using valid credentials
      Given I am on the login screen
      When I enter "Username" into the user field
      And I enter "PWD" into the password field
      And I click the login button
      Then I must see my user account
```

Listing 5.5 shows the Ruby code needed to map the real text into commands that the computer needs to understand in order to communicate and interact with the app.

Listing 5.5 *Sample Step Definition Code for One Gherkin Step*

```
When(/^I enter "(.*?)" into the user field$/)
do | username |
      fill_in("IDUserName", :with => "username")
end
```

As you can see, actual test automation is performed with Ruby and within the so-called step definitions. Gherkin is responsible for describing the behavior of the application, Ruby is needed for the actual coding, and Cucumber is the framework that executes everything together on the real devices or emulators. The Calabash tests can be executed from the command line, from an IDE, or from a continuous integration server.

Calabash supports a screenshot function, is able to use localization within the app, and supports different gestures.

Additional useful information about Calabash, Gherkin, and Cucumber can be found on the GitHub project page:

- Calabash for Android (https://github.com/calabash/calabash-android)
- Predefined step definitions for Android (https://github.com/calabash/calabash-android/blob/master/ruby-gem/lib/calabash-android/canned_steps.md)

---

18. https://github.com/cucumber/cucumber/wiki/Gherkin

Appium

Appium[19] is an open-source, cross-platform test automation tool for native, hybrid, and mobile Web apps. Appium supports the mobile platforms Android, iOS, and FirefoxOS. Like Selendroid, Appium uses the WebDriver JSON Wire Protocol to drive and to test the UI of the mobile apps. You can use several programming languages to write your test automation. Currently, Appium supports the following languages:

- C#
- Clojure
- Java
- JavaScript
- Objective-C
- Perl
- PHP
- Python
- Ruby

The written tests can be executed by emulators/simulators or real devices. The code in Listing 5.6 shows some of the test steps.

Listing 5.6 *Sample Appium Code*

```
WebElement loginText = driver.findElement(By.name("TextLogin"));
assertEquals("TextLogin", loginText.getText());
WebElement loginTextView =
  driver.findElementByClassName("android.widget.TextView");
assertEquals("TextLogin", loginTextView.getText());
WebElement button =
  driver.findElement(By.name("Login"));
button.click();
```

One of the main advantages of Appium is that the tool not only is able to communicate with the app being tested but is also able to start another app from the app under test, such as the camera app or the contacts app. Besides that, the app under test will not be modified when using Appium in order to automate it.

---

19. http://appium.io/

More information about Appium can be found on the GitHub page as well as on the manufacturer's page:

- Appium on GitHub (https://github.com/appium/appium)
- Appium introduction (http://appium.io/introduction.html)
- Appium API reference documentation (http://appium.io/slate/en/master)

Espresso

Espresso[20] is the Android test kit provided by Google. Espresso is based on an improved Instrumentation Test Runner called Google Instrumentation Test Runner[21] to make Android test automation more reliable and faster.

Espresso provides a small and easy-to-learn API to interact with the UI elements of a native Android app. Espresso is mainly aimed at developers who have access to the code base in order to write fast and reliable tests. However, if you are able to write Java code and have access to the code base of the app you want to test, Espresso is a nice little tool for writing the test automation. As an example, please refer to the code in Listing 5.7.

Listing 5.7 *Sample Code from Espresso*

```
onView(withId(R.id.login)).perform(click());
onView(withId(R.id.logout)).check(doesNotExist());
onView(withId(R.id.input)).perform(typeText("Hello"));
```

Espresso is able to execute tests either from the command line, from an IDE, or from a continuous integration server on real devices or emulators but not in parallel. However, test execution is much faster compared to that of any other Android test automation tools.

Additional useful information about Espresso can be found on the Google project page:

- Espresso start guide (https://code.google.com/p/android-test-kit/wiki/EspressoStartGuide)
- Espresso samples (https://code.google.com/p/android-test-kit/wiki/EspressoSamples)

---

20. https://code.google.com/p/android-test-kit/wiki/Espresso
21. https://code.google.com/p/android-test-kit/wiki/GoogleInstrumentationTestRunner

More Android Testing Tools

As I said at the beginning of this chapter, the list of Android test automation tools mentioned in this book is by no means complete. There are so many open- and closed-source tools available on the market, and more tools are bound to follow. The following list contains the names of some other Android test automation tools that you should try. This list contains some closed-source enterprise tools as well as some unit testing tools.

- eggPlant (www.testplant.com/eggplant/)
- Experitest (http://experitest.com/)
- Jamo Solutions (www.jamosolutions.com/)
- Keynote (www.keynote.com/solutions/testing/mobile-testing)
- MonkeyTalk (www.cloudmonkeymobile.com/monkeytalk)
- Perfecto Mobile (www.perfectomobile.com/)
- Ranorex (www.ranorex.com/)
- Robolectric (http://robolectric.org/)
- Siesta (https://market.sencha.com/extensions/siesta)
- Silk Mobile (www.borland.com/products/silkmobile/)
- SOASTA (www.soasta.com/products/soasta-platform/)
- TenKod EZ TestApp (www.tenkod.com/ez-testapp/)
- TestObject (https://testobject.com/)
- UI Automator (http://developer.android.com/tools/help/uiautomator/index.html)

Android Tool Recommendation

Recommending a mobile test automation tool is not easy. There are so many factors that need to be considered when choosing a mobile test automation tool, and those factors are different for each app and project. From my point of view and judging from the apps I have worked with (social media and booking apps), I recommend taking a closer look at Robotium, Spoon, Appium, and Selendroid.

All of the tools are great to work with. They offer full support for native, hybrid, and Web-based apps. Besides that, all of the tools come with good documentation, code samples, and a great community if you want to ask questions. And last but not least, writing test code with the tools is very easy and lots of fun.

When choosing Robotium as a test automation tool, I highly recommend combining it with Spoon. Spoon's test reporting feature is excellent, and the option to run your tests on several devices at the same time is unbeatable. Robotium is a well-developed Android test automation tool with a huge community and lots of support behind it.

Appium and Selendroid are also tools you should keep in mind. Both offer a great way to develop your automated tests in several programming languages. Both tools have great options for scaling your testing process in a cloud or a Selenium Grid.

> **Important**   Keep one thing in mind: No matter which tool you use for test automation, use the resource IDs of the UI components if possible as doing so speeds up test automation and makes it more reliable.

iOS Tools

Let's go further with some iOS testing tools. What I already mentioned for the Android tools also applies to iOS tools:

- The selected tool list is not complete.
- I have included end-to-end test automation tools.
- All mentioned tools require coding skills.
- Before you start with iOS test automation, make sure you're familiar with the iOS UI structure of iOS apps.

UI Automation

UI Automation[22] is the iOS testing tool that is part of Instruments[23] provided by Apple. With the help of UI Automation, you are able to either record the tests or write them manually using JavaScript. If you are familiar with iOS apps, you know that iOS apps use so-called accessibility labels to describe the UI elements and make them accessible, such as for screen readers. Most iOS testing tools and UI Automation use these accessibility labels in order to communicate and interact with the app being tested. If your app has no defined accessibility labels, you are not able to write test automation for it.

---

22. https://developer.apple.com/library/mac/documentation/DeveloperTools/Conceptual/
    InstrumentsUserGuide/UsingtheAutomationInstrument/UsingtheAutomationInstrument.html
23. https://developer.apple.com/library/ios/documentation/DeveloperTools/Conceptual/
    InstrumentsUserGuide/Introduction/Introduction.html

UI Automation is able to simulate real user interactions such as tap, swipe, scroll, pinch, or type, either on a real device or on the iOS simulator. The code in Listing 5.8 shows some test actions that can be performed.

Listing 5.8 *Sample Code from UI Automation*

```
app.keyboard().typeString("Some text");
rootTable.cells()["List Entry 7"].tap();
alert.buttons()["Continue"].tap();
```

UI Automation is able to change the device orientation from portrait to landscape mode and back again. It is also able to handle different alerts that may occur during the test run on the mobile device. The automated tests can be executed from the command line, within the IDE, and from a continuous integration server.

More information about UI Automation can be found on Apple's developer pages:

- UI Automation JavaScript reference (https://developer.apple.com/library/ios/documentation/DeveloperTools/Reference/UIAutomationRef/_index .html)

Calabash for iOS

Calabash[24] is a cross-platform mobile test automation framework for native and hybrid Android and iOS apps (if you have already read about it in the Android section, you can skip ahead). The tool enables automated UI acceptance tests written in Cucumber.[25] With the help of Cucumber, you can express the behavior of the app you're testing using a natural language. This approach is called behavior-driven development (BDD), and it can be very helpful when business experts or nontechnical colleagues are involved in the acceptance criteria process.

> **Important**   I already described the features of Calabash in the Android tools section, so please refer back there. Almost exactly the same process is involved when writing the feature and step definition files for Android and iOS.

---

24. http://calaba.sh/
25. http://cukes.info/

To get more information about Calabash for iOS, check out the Calabash iOS project site:

- Calabash for iOS (https://github.com/calabash/calabash-ios)
- Getting started with Calabash for iOS (https://github.com/calabash/calabash-ios/wiki/01-Getting-started-guide)
- Predefined steps for Calabash iOS (https://github.com/calabash/calabash-ios/wiki/02-Predefined-steps)

ios-driver

ios-driver[26] is able to automate native iOS, hybrid, and mobile Web apps using the Selenium WebDriver API. It uses the same approach as Selendroid but for iOS apps. It implements the JSON Wire Protocol in order to communicate and test iOS apps using Instruments. The tool is able to execute the tests either on a real device or on a simulator. Like Appium and Selendroid, ios-driver offers you a different set of programming languages with which you can write your test scripts. You can choose from the following:

- C#
- Clojure
- Java
- JavaScript
- Objective-C
- Perl
- PHP
- Python
- Ruby

The code in Listing 5.9 shows some of the possible test commands for a native iOS app written in Java.

Listing 5.9 *Sample Code from ios-driver*

```
By button = By.id("Login");
WebElement loginButton = driver.findElement(button);
Assert.assertEquals(loginButton.getAttribute("name"), "Login");
loginButton.click();
```

---

26. http://ios-driver.github.io/ios-driver/

In order to identify the UI elements of the app, ios-driver provides a UI inspector[27] similar to Selendroid that identifies and views the properties of the UI elements. ios-driver is able to handle localized apps and doesn't require any changes to the app under test. The tests can be executed from the command line or from a continuous integration server. Furthermore, the tool can be used as a node within a Selenium Grid to scale and parallelize the testing.

More information about ios-driver can be found on the manufacturer's Web site, as well as on the GitHub project page:

- ios-driver getting started (http://ios-driver.github.io/ios-driver/?page=setup)
- Source code and samples (https://github.com/ios-driver/ios-driver)

Keep It Functional

Keep It Functional[28] (KIF) is an open-source iOS testing tool developed by the company Square.[29] KIF is able to automate native iOS apps using the accessibility labels provided by the app. This tool uses the so-called `tester` object to be able to simulate user inputs such as touch, swipe, scroll, and typing. Objective-C is used to write automated test scripts for KIF, and KIF is able to execute the tests on a real device or iOS simulator.

Have a look at the sample code of Keep It Functional shown in Listing 5.10.

Listing 5.10 *Sample Code from Keep It Functional*

```
[tester enterText:@"user one" intoViewWithAccessibilityLabel: @"User
Name"];
[tester enterText:@"Mypassword" intoViewWithAccessibilityLabel:
@"Login  Password"];
[tester tapViewWithAccessibilityLabel:@"Login"];
```

KIF can be fully integrated within Xcode to start and debug the test automation scripts. Furthermore, the automated tests can be executed from the command line or from a continuous integration server such as Bots.[30]

There's one thing you need to keep in mind when automating tests with KIF: it uses undocumented Apple APIs. This is not a problem when testing an app, but it's crucial that your test scripts not be part of the production code. If they are, Apple will reject your app due to the use of undocumented APIs. If you follow KIF's installation instructions, this should not be an issue.

---

27. http://ios-driver.github.io/ios-driver/?page=inspector
28. https://github.com/kif-framework/KIF
29. http://corner.squareup.com/2011/07/ios-integration-testing.html
30. https://developer.apple.com/library/ios/documentation/IDEs/Conceptual/xcode_guide-continuous_
    integration/ConfigureBots/ConfigureBots.html

Appium

Appium[31] is an open-source, cross-platform test automation tool for native, hybrid, and mobile Web apps (if you have already read about it in the Android section, you can skip ahead). Appium supports the mobile platforms Android, iOS, and FirefoxOS. Like Selendroid, Appium uses the WebDriver JSON Wire Protocol to drive and test the UI of the mobile apps.

> **Important**   I already described the features of Appium in the Android tools section, so please refer back there.

More iOS Testing Tools

As I did for Android, I'd like to provide you with a list of additional iOS testing tools. The following list contains unit testing and end-to-end open- and closed-source testing tools; it is by no means complete:

- Experitest (http://experitest.com/)
- Frank (www.testingwithfrank.com/)
- GHUnit (https://github.com/gh-unit/gh-unit)
- Jamo Solutions (www.jamosolutions.com/)
- Keynote (www.keynote.com/solutions/testing/mobile-testing)
- Kiwi (https://github.com/kiwi-bdd/Kiwi)
- MonkeyTalk (www.cloudmonkeymobile.com/monkeytalk)
- OCMock (http://ocmock.org/)
- Perfecto Mobile (www.perfectomobile.com/)
- Ranorex (www.ranorex.com/)
- Silk Mobile (www.borland.com/products/silkmobile/)
- SOASTA (www.soasta.com/products/soasta-platform/)
- Specta (https://github.com/specta/specta)
- Subliminal (https://github.com/inkling/Subliminal)
- XCTest (https://developer.apple.com/library/prerelease/ios/documentation/ DeveloperTools/Conceptual/testing_with_xcode/testing_2_testing_basics/ testing_2_testing_basics.html#//apple_ref/doc/uid/TP40014132-CH3-SW3)
- Zucchini (www.zucchiniframework.org/)

---

31. http://appium.io/

iOS Tool Recommendation

Recommending an iOS test automation tool is also not an easy task. Just as for Android, there are so many factors to consider when choosing an iOS test automation tool. I recommend that you take a closer look at ios-driver, Appium, and Keep It Functional.

All of the tools provide really good and powerful features in order to build reliable and robust test automation scripts for iOS apps. If you just want to automate a native iOS app, KIF would be a good choice as you can set up and write reliable and robust automated tests very quickly. Another advantage of KIF is that the test scripts are written with Objective-C, the same language with which the app will be written. If you struggle with Objective-C, you can simply ask your developers for support or have them write the test automation.

If you want to automate a hybrid iOS or Web app, you should use either ios-driver or Appium as both offer great support for various programming languages as well as the option to use them in a cloud or Selenium Grid environment. This provides powerful scaling and parallel test execution on several different devices and operating systems.

All three tools come with good documentation and very good code samples, are easy to use, and have a huge community behind them that is on hand to help if you run into any problems.

Mobile Test Automation Tools Summary

As you have seen, there are many different mobile test automation frameworks available on the market. Each tool has its own style of writing test scripts and supports different feature sets, different mobile platforms, and different mobile app types. Every tool currently available on the market has its pros and cons. You should really keep in mind that no tool is perfect, be it an open- or closed-source tool. Before selecting a mobile test automation tool, scan the market for possible tools and solutions to help you make the right decision. Use a sample app or a checklist to evaluate the various tools.

And last but not least, it's important to start simple with a mobile test automation tool. Don't try and find THE one and only test automation solution for your mobile app. Maybe you need to use more than one tool or to combine tools in order to build up a test automation suite that covers your needs and requirements. It is better to have only a certain amount of test automation in place that covers, for example, the critical parts of your app instead of every part. When choosing a tool, ask yourself the question "What should be automated?"

Continuous Integration System

Continuous integration (CI) is nothing new, and this development practice of integrating and testing the code from a centrally shared code repository several times a day has been in use for several years now. Every check-in is then verified by a different set of automated build steps to ensure that the latest code changes will not break the software and integration with other modules.

A CI server should be available in every project, no matter if the software is a desktop, Web, or mobile application, as it will help the team reduce the risk of broken software, give fast feedback to everyone involved in the project, and integrate smaller software parts into others as early as possible within the process.

Nowadays, there are plenty of open- and closed-source CI systems available on the market. If you have a CI system in your team, integrate the automated mobile tests into it. Nearly every mobile test automation tool can be integrated into a CI system. If this is not possible with the tool you're using, you'll have to find a way to integrate it such as with external build scripts that will run outside the CI environment to fulfill the task. This is very important for the project as a whole so that a complete build pipeline including all build and test scripts can be established.

When the test automation tool has been integrated, define a build and test strategy with your team. Talk to your developers and define which tests should be executed after every commit or during the night.

If your automated tests start to turn fast feedback from your CI system into slow feedback, split them into separate test suites. For example, you can define a smoke test suite containing tests that check whether the main parts of the application are still working. This test suite runs for only a couple of seconds or minutes and should be executed after every commit. Another test suite can be a regression test suite that runs, say, four times a day to check the app in more detail. And another suite can be a full test suite that runs every test every night to make sure the code changes from the previous day have not affected the existing parts of the app.

Another important point when adding a mobile test automation tool to a CI system is test reporting. The CI system must be able to display different kinds of test report formats in order to provide the whole team with visual feedback. The reporting component of the system should be easy to read and understand.

Once the CI system and all of the mobile testing and development tools have been integrated, define a complete build and test pipeline for your mobile application. The build pipeline should be able to start automatically without any user inputs, for example, by either listening to a central code repository or triggering the builds at a certain time during the night.

Furthermore, the build steps should trigger other build steps in order to unit-test, end-to-end-test, build an application on different staging systems, build alpha or beta versions of the app, or upload the application to a beta distribution server.

Here is an example of a possible, very simple mobile build pipeline:

1. Perform static code analysis, such as with PMD, FindBugs, Lint, or Checkstyle.

2. Perform unit tests.

3. Perform end-to-end UI tests.

4. Build a mobile app version on different staging systems.

5. Build a beta version of the mobile app.

6. Upload the beta version to a beta distribution system.

7. Sign and build a release candidate of the app (the only build step that should be triggered manually).

Build steps 1 and 2 should be executed on the developer's computer before he or she commits the code to the central repository.

If you have a CI system for your mobile app in place, don't forget to plug real devices into that server in order to execute all of the test automation on the real device.

The following are some of the available CI systems:

- Bamboo (www.atlassian.com/de/software/bamboo)
- Bots (https://developer.apple.com/library/ios/documentation/IDEs/ Conceptual/xcode_guide-continuous_integration/ConfigureBots/ ConfigureBots.html)
- Buildbot (http://buildbot.net/)
- CruiseControl (http://cruisecontrol.sourceforge.net/)
- Janky (https://github.com/github/janky)
- Jenkins (http://jenkins-ci.org/)
- TeamCity (www.jetbrains.com/teamcity/)
- Travis CI (https://travis-ci.org/)

> **Important**   Have a CI system in place and integrate your mobile test automation tool to get fast feedback about the quality of the app after every code change.

Beta Distribution Tools

As you have learned from the previous chapters, mobile users have expectations in terms of the usability, performance, and features of mobile apps. You and your team therefore have to be sure that your mobile app provides a great user experience and is fast, reliable, and fun to use. To meet all of these expectations, you and your team have a challenging job and need to test the app with other people to get feedback as early as possible in the development process.

To get this feedback from other users such as colleagues or users from your target customer group, you need a tool to distribute beta versions of your app. With the help of this tool, you can give potential users access to a beta version of the next release candidate.

Beta distribution tools include several useful features such as over-the-air app distribution, crash reporting, bug reporting, and direct in-app feedback. Some tools provide so-called checkpoints within the app where you can place questions for the user about the feature he or she just used. Another nice feature is so-called sessions, which can be included to track how the beta tester uses the app or a feature, thus helping you to identify unexpected app usage. The tools also provide data and statistics about the mobile operating system versions, device hardware, and interface language.

All of the information provided by a beta distribution tool is really important to know before your app is used by the majority of your target customer group. You can draw on this information to refine and develop your app in the right direction, thus making it far more reliable, stable, and of course fun to use.

When using a beta distribution tool, it is very important to inform the potential beta testers about all of these features and that information is gathered about the device and the user.

As a starting point, use a beta distribution tool within your company by asking your colleagues to test the app and provide feedback. Not every mobile app can be distributed as a beta version to the outside world due to network restrictions, company guidelines, or pertinent law.

Here is a list of beta distribution tools:

- Appaloosa (www.appaloosa-store.com/)
- AppBlade (https://appblade.com/)
- Applause SDK (www.applause.com/mobile-sdk)
- Beta by Crashlytics (http://try.crashlytics.com/beta/)
- BirdFlight (www.birdflightapp.com/)
- Google Play native App Beta Testing (https://play.google.com/apps/publish)
- HockeyApp (http://hockeyapp.net/)

- HockeyKit (http://hockeykit.net/)
- TestFlight (https://developer.apple.com/testflight/index.html)

Google and Apple also provide a way to distribute a beta app version to a wider user base. Within Google Play[32] you are able to add beta testers with their Gmail addresses who can then download the beta version from the Google Play store. Alternatively, you can define a staged rollout where a new version of your app is available only to a certain number of users, for example, 10% of the current user base. If the app works as expected, you can increase the app rollout either to your entire user base or by another increment.

On the Apple[33] side, you are also able to build a beta version of your app and distribute it to registered beta testers. The beta testers have to be registered with their unique device ID (UDID) using an ad hoc provisioning profile. However, you are able to register only 100 test devices within one membership year. You can get around this test device restriction if your company is part of Apple's enterprise program.

> **Important** Wherever possible, use a beta distribution tool to gather early feedback from beta testers in order to build a better mobile app.

Summary

The fifth chapter of this book concentrated on mobile test automation. At the beginning of the chapter I explained the problem with the traditional test automation pyramid and mobile apps. I introduced and explained the flipped testing pyramid and showed a new pyramid—the mobile test pyramid. This pyramid contains automated, as well as manual, testing to fit all the requirements of the current state for mobile apps.

In the next section of this chapter I described the different approaches and types of mobile test automation tools. These are tools that use image recognition, coordinate-based recognition, text recognition, or native object recognition. I explained every approach, with pros and cons. Furthermore, I assigned the available tools on the market to the different approaches to provide you with an overview.

In another section I explained why it is a bad idea to just use capture and replay tools for your test automation. Those tools do provide a good starting

32. https://support.google.com/googleplay/android-developer/answer/3131213?hl=en
33. https://developer.apple.com/library/ios/documentation/IDEs/Conceptual/AppDistributionGuide/TestingYouriOSApp/TestingYouriOSApp.html

point to get some test automation up and running in the first place, but in the long run they will cause lots of maintenance trouble and the tests aren't reliable at all.

In the section "What Should Be Automated?" I explained which parts of your app need test automation and which do not. For example, it is a good approach to automate the business-critical parts of the app. On the other hand, those parts that are likely to change often in the near future are fine for manual testing because the test automation will not run in a stable fashion if they are included.

To help you select the right test automation tool for your mobile app, I included a list with selection criteria to find the tool that fits best into your development and test environment.

The biggest part of this chapter covered the current state of mobile test automation tools for the iOS and Android platforms. I explained the different tools with code samples as well as pros and cons. I described the following tools:

- Robotium
- Spoon
- Selendroid
- Calabash for Android and iOS
- Appium
- Espresso
- UI Automation
- ios-driver
- Keep It Functional

The closing sections of this chapter covered the topics of continuous integration and beta distribution of mobile apps. I outlined a sample mobile CI build pipeline that can easily be adapted to your environment. I added a list of CI tools that can be used for mobile apps. In the beta distribution section, I explained the purpose of distributing a beta version of your app to colleagues or beta testers to get early feedback and bug reports.

Chapter 6

Additional Mobile Testing Methods

So far you've learned about mobile technologies and how to manually test mobile apps in different scenarios as well as while out and about. You've learned about mobile test automation and the concepts behind the different mobile test automation tools. You're now aware of several tools for the different mobile platforms and know how to select the right tool for your testing process.

To extend your knowledge and your toolbox, in this chapter I introduce some other possible mobile testing approaches: crowd and cloud testing. Both of these approaches can be beneficial in your daily work within a mobile team.

Crowd Testing

A company has three possible ways to establish software testing within an organization. Testing can be done with the aid of an in-house quality assurance department, via outsourcing (nearshoring/offshoring), or using a crowd testing approach. In-house testing and outsourcing are nothing new, and both are considered established approaches among various organizations and industries.

But this is not the case with crowd testing. The term *crowdsourcing* was introduced by Jee Howe[1] in 2006 and is a combination of the words *crowd* and *outsourcing*. In the software testing business the word *crowdsourcing* has become *crowd testing*.

---

1. www.crowdsourcing.com/

With the help of a community of external software testers, several crowd testing providers offer a new way to perform software testing. The external software testers come from diverse backgrounds, both geographically and in terms of their level of technical knowledge. Depending on the crowd testing provider, the crowd can range from a few people to several thousand testers worldwide, and it may include software testing experts and people of any age, gender, profession, and educational background. Furthermore, the crowd testers have lots of different devices with diverse hardware and software combinations and access to a number of different data networks. Crowd testing is tantamount to testing in the wild.

With the aid of crowd testers, an app will be tested under a set of realistic scenarios that can't be created by an in-house testing team. The mobile app will be tested under real-world conditions—with different data networks, hardware, and software as well as different users. External testers provide a fresh set of eyes for your mobile app and will doubtless report lots of bugs, deviations, as well as performance, usability, and functional issues.

Crowd testing providers offer a platform where crowd testers can register and create a profile stating their devices, skills, and demographic background. The client can add the app under test, the preconditions, sample scenarios, instructions, known bugs, and detailed test plans. The client is also able to define the demographic background, target customer group, skill set, and devices on which the crowd should test the mobile app.

Some crowd providers have a project management framework in place, including governance and legal structures for the testing phase. In addition, test providers assign a project manager who is responsible for the test cycle. The project manager is also the person who filters, rates, and categorizes the bugs reported by the crowd and summarizes the testing cycle for the client.

Some crowd testing providers have an assessment center or trial project in place where possible crowd testers must participate in order to verify their testing abilities before being accepted into the testing community.

Most crowd testing providers charge a fee for their services, but crowd testing is relatively cheap because you pay only for the package that you have agreed upon with the crowd testing provider. There are different kinds of packages available, such as simple bug reporting, exploratory testing, and/or executing defined test cases.

Figure 6.1 shows the typical crowd testing process from the first briefing with the crowd provider to the final presentation. During the test cycle, the client is always able to see the live progress of the crowd testers.

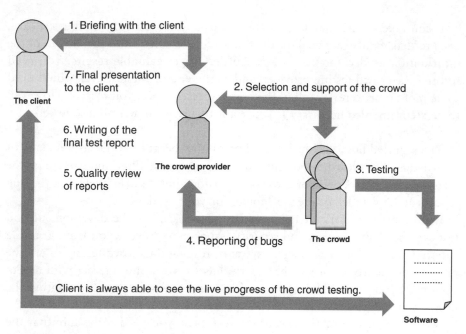

Figure 6.1 *Typical crowd testing process*

1. The first step is the initial briefing between the crowd provider and the client.

2. The crowd provider selects the crowd based on the client's requirements. During the test cycle the provider supports the crowd.

3. The crowd tests the software.

4. The crowd testers file reports depending on the aim of the test cycle, for example, bugs, feedback, or any other kind of problems.

5. The crowd provider ensures that the quality of the reports is good enough. He or she will follow up on bugs if more information is needed.

6. At the end of the test cycle the crowd provider writes the final test report.

7. The report is then presented to the client.

However, there are some challenges you need to be aware of if you want to use a crowd testing approach in your project.

It can take a long time to prepare and organize a crowd testing cycle. You need to define the exact goal for the test cycle and collect and prepare all of the information needed for the crowd in order to get valuable results. You need to brief the crowd testing provider, and at the end of the test cycle you'll need some more time to review all of the bug and test reports you receive. However, these steps are also necessary if you want to brief a new in-house tester on a new project.

The reported bugs may be of very low quality because of the crowd's lack of knowledge. The crowd testing provider will of course filter and categorize the bugs and pay testers only for those of real value, but it's also likely that the bug reports aren't detailed or precise enough for your needs.

It may be very difficult for crowd testers to access the development and test systems. Data privacy and security issues may prevent you from granting external access to internal staging systems, forcing the crowd testers to use the production environment which, in turn, has to work and interact with a beta version of your app. Maybe you need to create an isolated section within the production environment that can handle the beta requests and be used for the crowd testing cycle. At the end of the test cycle you need to be sure that the crowd testers are no longer able to access the production environment and that the app will be of no use to them.

Another challenge comes in the form of legal hurdles and NDAs (nondisclosure agreements). If your app is confidential, for example, crowd testing may simply not be an option.

The pros of crowd testing include the following:

- The crowd includes different testers from around the world, with different demographic backgrounds and skill sets.
- Lots of different mobile devices with different hardware and software combinations can be used for testing.
- The mobile app is tested in real-world conditions with real users.
- The crowd provides a fresh set of eyes for your application.
- Lots of issues will be reported.
- Crowd testing providers filter and categorize the bugs.

The cons of crowd testing include the following:

- Crowd testers are not generally testing experts.
- You don't really know whom you're dealing with.
- Bug reports may be of low quality.

- Access to staging systems can be very difficult due to legal hurdles, data privacy, and security concerns.
- Crowd testing can take a long time to prepare.
- Communication with the crowd can be difficult.
- Reproducing bugs can be difficult.
- There is a risk that the mobile app will continue to be used by the crowd after the test cycle has ended.

Important   Some crowd testing providers have a mechanism to automatically uninstall the app under test from testers' mobile devices.

The following list includes some crowd testing providers (this list is by no means complete):

- 99tests (http://99tests.com/)
- Applause (www.applause.com/)
- crowdsourcedtesting (https://crowdsourcedtesting.com)
- Global App Testing (http://globalapptesting.com/)
- Mob4Hire (www.mob4hire.com/)
- passbrains (www.passbrains.com/)
- Testbirds (www.testbirds.de/)
- testCloud (www.testcloud.io/)
- TestPlus (www.testplus.at/)

Important   The crowd testing approach is a good extension of your in-house testing team. However, crowd testing won't and shouldn't replace your in-house testing activities.

Private Crowd Testing

If you're not able to use a public crowd testing provider because of legal restrictions, NDAs, or data privacy and data security concerns, or because you're not able to grant access to your development environment, you can use a private crowd testing approach.

You can start and build up an internal crowd testing session with your colleagues. Depending on the size of your company, you'll be surrounded by lots of people from different backgrounds working in various departments, so you can collect feedback from developers, designers, product managers, project managers, management, sales, and marketing colleagues. With the input from your colleagues, you'll be able to simulate real users in different usage scenarios to get an initial impression of your app.

One of the biggest advantages you'll notice when establishing a private crowd testing approach is that you'll need less time to prepare and organize it than with a public crowd testing approach because your colleagues are already familiar with the corporate environment, the product, and its features. Employees can also gain access to the development or staging environment, which allows you to sidestep any legal restrictions and NDAs.

Furthermore, it is very easy to communicate with your colleagues during the test cycle and to observe them while they are using the app. This will provide you and your team with extremely valuable insights into how users actually interact with your app in terms of usability and functionality. At the end of a test cycle you can interview your colleagues about the app and its new features to gather more information about their opinions of the app and any problems they encountered during testing.

The internal crowd testing session can be kept short and can be repeated several times during your app's development phase. This gives you more flexibility when it comes to reacting to possible usability, functional, or performance problems.

One way to keep your colleagues dedicated and motivated is to introduce your internal testing session as a competition. Try creating categories for the competition and award prizes for each category. Possible categories could include the following:

- Best usability bug
- Best functional bug
- Best performance bug
- Best security bug
- Best feedback provided
- Best bug report
- Best overall test engagement

Prizes could include the following:

- Company mugs
- Funny stickers

- T-shirts with funny slogans
- Vouchers

Prizes don't have to be expensive; they just need to motivate people to find and report as many bugs as possible. Furthermore, competition will give your colleagues an incentive to take part in upcoming test cycles.

Important   Try to create a private crowd testing session within your company and see how your colleagues perform as testers. You'll be surprised at the bugs and the reported results.

Mobile Cloud Testing

Manufacturers of mobile cloud testing solutions provide a wide range of current mobile devices with different hardware and software combinations in the cloud. Cloud testing providers use the characteristics of cloud computing to provide this service to mobile companies, teams, and mobile testers. Such characteristics include the following:

- The cloud uses a dynamic, shared, and virtual IT infrastructure.
- The cloud provides on-demand self-service.
- The cloud is scalable based on the load.
- The cloud is priced according to consumption.
- The cloud is available across different network connections.

Mobile cloud testing solutions are accessible via the Web and provide different types of testing that can be performed within the cloud on real or emulated/simulated devices. The different testing types available are:

- Functional testing
- Performance testing
- Load testing
- Mobile device testing
- Cross-browser testing

As is the case with Open Device Labs, the mobile cloud provides you and your team with easy access to a comprehensive range of current mobile devices using all of the different mobile platforms, no matter where you are in the world. If you want to test your mobile app in the cloud, all you need to do is allocate the physical device, upload and install your app, and start your manual or automated testing. Providers offer different kinds of additional services such as reporting features, screenshots, and videos of your test session or an API to execute your test automation scripts on several devices in parallel.

The fact that mobile test clouds are distributed in different geographical regions all over the world makes it easy to simulate different network technologies and scenarios from potential mobile users.

One major advantage of a mobile test cloud is that you don't need to buy new phones for your development or testing efforts as this will be done by the cloud provider. Furthermore, you don't need to maintain all the different devices, which may have a positive impact on your project costs.

However, there are also some limitations if you want to test your mobile app within a mobile cloud. For example, if your app uses a Bluetooth connection to connect to other physical elements such as speakers, it is not possible to test within a cloud. It is also not possible to use all the sensors and interfaces such as the proximity sensor, brightness sensor, acceleration sensor, or gyroscope sensor because the cloud devices are mounted and connected to a server within a data center. On top of that, you can't test your mobile app for interruptions or notifications from other apps or the device itself.

Another drawback of testing your app manually within a mobile cloud is that you're interacting with your app through the computer mouse. You have no physical contact with the device or app with your hand or fingers, making it very difficult to get a feel for the usability and response of the app. Furthermore, multitouch gestures can't be performed on the touch interface.

And, last but not least, security and privacy issues shouldn't be underestimated when using a mobile test cloud. You need to be sure that the provider will completely remove your app and its data from the test devices after the test session has been completed; otherwise the next cloud testing user might be able to see and use your app.

Before choosing a mobile cloud testing provider, check the provided features and compare them with those of other vendors. You should also weigh the pros and cons of mobile cloud testing to see if this approach fits your project and development environment.

The pros of mobile cloud testing include the following:

- Easy access to the physical devices
- Easy access to emulators and simulators
- Fast and easy setup of the mobile devices

- Accessibility from anywhere in the world
- Lower costs as there's no need to buy new devices
- No device maintenance costs
- Different test types
- Simulated network providers from all over the world
- Good reporting features such as reports, screenshots, and videos

The cons of mobile cloud testing include the following:

- You have less control over the mobile devices.
- Network issues can affect the availability and the functionality of the mobile test cloud.
- Security and privacy issues: Other companies use the same devices, so you need to be sure the app will be deleted in full after the session has been completed.
- Performance problems: Testing the app via the Internet can have an impact on the app execution time and test results.
- Firewall setup: You need to change some of the firewall settings in order to gain access to the development and test environments.
- If the cloud has any system problems or outages, your app test environment may also experience poor performance or outages.
- It is difficult to track down intermittent problems because you have no access to the system.
- Not everything can be tested within a cloud, for example, sensors, interfaces, interrupts, and notifications.
- You have no physical contact with the device.

The following are some mobile cloud testing providers (this list is by no means complete):

- AppThwack (https://appthwack.com/)
- Appurify (http://appurify.com/)
- CloudMonkey (www.cloudmonkeymobile.com/)
- Experitest (http://experitest.com/cloud/)
- Keynote (www.keynote.com/)
- Neotys (www.neotys.com/product/neotys-cloud-platform.html)

- Perfecto Mobile (www.perfectomobile.com/)
- Ranorex (www.ranorex.com/)
- Sauce Labs (https://saucelabs.com/)
- TestChameleon (www.testchameleon.com/)
- Testdroid (http://testdroid.com/)
- Testmunk (www.testmunk.com/)
- TestObject (https://testobject.com/)
- Xamarin Test Cloud (http://xamarin.com/test-cloud)

> **Important** Mobile cloud testing is a good extension to your in-house testing work but comes with some testing limitations that need to be taken into consideration.

Private Cloud

If the drawbacks outweigh the advantages of a public cloud, but you're still interested in using a cloud testing approach, consider using a private mobile testing cloud. Almost every provider in the preceding list can provide a private mobile test cloud.

A private mobile cloud can be offered as a hosted or locally installed solution. The hosted solution is the more common one because it eliminates the logistics and costs incurred by buying new phones and maintaining devices, such as installing updates and performing configurations. Private cloud providers offer a secure area within the data center that grants exclusive access to the physical devices. On top of that, they offer various security options to meet a company's security policies and requirements.

The locally installed solution is also known as a private mobile test lab. If you decide to use this solution, the mobile cloud provider will provide you with a mobile testing rack including device management software to maintain and allocate test devices within your company to developers or testers. You can also extend the rack with new devices on your own.

This device rack will be located behind your firewall, and devices are connected to the development environment, which alleviates any problems with the speed and connection problems of a public cloud. Security and privacy concerns are also no longer an issue with this solution. By way of example, refer to the mobile test lab from Mobile Labs.[2]

---

2. http://mobilelabsinc.com/products/deviceconnect/

A locally installed solution also comes with the problem that you're responsible for buying and maintaining new devices to be included in the device rack. Furthermore, a private mobile testing cloud can be really expensive as you have exclusive access to the test devices, the cloud vendor provides you with exclusive support, and both you and your company need to train your colleagues to be able to work with the private cloud software and system.

The pros of a private mobile test cloud include the following:

- Easy access to the physical devices
- Fast and easy setup of the mobile devices
- Accessibility from anywhere in the world
- No device maintenance costs (hosted solution only)
- Different test types
- Simulation of various network providers from all over the world (hosted solution only)
- Exclusive access to the test devices
- No security concerns

The cons of a private mobile test cloud include the following:

- It is far more expensive than a public mobile test cloud.
- Network issues can still affect the availability and the functionality of the mobile test cloud.
- Firewall setup: You need to change some firewall settings to gain access to the development and test environments (hosted solution only).
- If the cloud has any system problems or outages, your app will perform poorly and may also experience outages (hosted solution only).
- It is difficult to track down intermittent problems because you have no access to the system (hosted solution only).
- Not everything can be tested within a cloud, for example, sensors and interfaces.
- Additional training is required to work with the cloud provider software and system.

> **Important**   Because of the manual testing limitations, you should consider using mobile test clouds for mobile test automation purposes only with the aim of handling automated testing and fragmentation across several devices. Manual testing should still be performed on real devices in real-world environments and while on the move.

Cloud-Based Test Automation

In Chapter 5, "Mobile Test Automation and Tools," I explained the different concepts of mobile test automation tools. I also described some mobile test automation tools for the iOS and Android platforms. When choosing a mobile test automation tool, check to see if the tool is able to execute the test scripts within a mobile test cloud. Some of the mobile test cloud providers offer an API for various mobile testing tools so you can execute your scripts with their services. This API can help you scale your testing efforts and test different devices in parallel. Some providers offer the possibility of writing test automation scripts on the Web within the cloud testing software.

The advantages of a mobile test cloud also apply to test automation within the cloud. A mobile test cloud can help you create an automated on-demand test environment for your mobile app and mobile platform.

However, using a cloud-based test automation approach also has some additional drawbacks. Test execution on cloud devices is slower than with a local test automation solution, which is partly due to the communication between the cloud provider network and your company network when requesting and sending lots of data. This latency can have an impact on the test results and behavior of your app. Testing the performance with test automation scripts on a mobile test cloud is therefore not an ideal solution. Debugging the test automation scripts on the cloud devices is another issue as script debugging is possible but not yet good enough to work efficiently.

If you're considering using a cloud-based test solution, evaluate several providers to see if they offer the features you need for your mobile app. A cloud-based test automation approach can be a useful addition to your in-house test automation and can make your testing work more efficient.

Summary

In the sixth chapter you have learned about crowd and cloud testing services. Both can be additions to your in-house mobile testing activities but should never be used as the only mobile testing solution for your app.

In the crowd testing section I explained the typical process of a crowd testing cycle. You need to keep in mind that this process will take quite some time for preparation as well as in the bug analysis phase. These efforts should not be underestimated. Furthermore, I described the differences between a private and a public crowd test session. Both approaches differ a lot in the details; however, those details are important in order to avoid infrastructure, data protection, and security concerns.

In the cloud testing section, I explained the features of a cloud testing provider. In addition, I described which test types can be performed within a cloud. In the pros and cons section I outlined possible problems with public and private clouds as well as the advantages.

Chapter 7

Mobile Test
and Launch Strategies

So far you've learned a lot about mobile testing and the different test techniques and approaches. This chapter covers mobile test and launch strategies and what you need to include in your strategies. Both the test and launch strategies are very important to every project, and you shouldn't underestimate just how useful it is to keep a written record of them. In the following sections I'll provide you with some examples of mobile test and launch strategies. You'll also find some questions that will help you to write your own strategies.

Mobile Test Strategy

In general, a test strategy is a document that describes the testing approach and work involved in the software development cycle. This strategy can be used to let the project manager, product manager, developers, designers, and anyone else involved in the software development cycle know about the key issues of the software testing process.

A test strategy includes the testing objective, test levels and techniques, resources required to test the system under test, and the testing environment. It also describes the product risks and how to mitigate them for stakeholders and customers. Finally, it also includes a definition of test entry and exit criteria.

The defined test strategy will help, remind, and guide you so you don't forget the important components and features of the app. You really should take the time to write down the steps and resources needed to test the mobile app. Furthermore, the test strategy documents your work and endeavors within the project. Writing a test strategy once doesn't mean that it's then set in stone and you can't make any subsequent changes. On the contrary, it's important that you talk about the strategy with your team from time to time so you can adapt it to any product changes or other more recent circumstances.

However, there is no single mobile test strategy that can be used by every team or for every mobile app as almost every app has different requirements, goals, and target groups and runs on different mobile platforms, which makes it impossible to reuse the entire strategy in every project. But there will, of course, be some items that can and should be reused.

The following sections of this chapter should give you an idea of how to shape a mobile test strategy. You can use them as a starting point and guide for putting together your own mobile test strategy.

> **Important**   Drafting a mobile test strategy doesn't necessarily involve writing endless documentation as you and any other testers simply won't have the time and/or the resources to run through it all, and flexibility is the name of the game in the mobile testing business. A mobile test strategy should serve to guide you and anyone else involved in the project so you can keep tabs on the important parts of the testing process.

Define Requirements

The first thing you and your team should do is define your app's requirements and features at the very beginning of the project. Write them all down and describe the features and possible use scenarios to get a better feeling for the app and its potential users. Rough descriptions of the requirements and features are absolutely fine at this point as they will be specified in more detail during the development process. A written record of these requirements will make it much easier for you to derive your mobile testing strategy.

Here is a list of some possible requirements and features:

- Provide a registration form.
- Provide a login form to access the app's content.
- Provide a logout option.
- Implement a search function within the app.
- The user should be able to create a user profile.
- The user should be able to share content with other users.
- The user should be able to share content on social networks.

- The user should be able to take pictures.
- The app should be available in different languages (English, German, French, and so on).

Furthermore, you should know who's going to use your app. As described in Chapter 3, "Challenges in Mobile Testing," you really need to know your target group and their expectations. Gather as much information as you can to gain important insights into your customers' use scenarios.

Here's a quick recap of possible information about your target group (the full list can be found in Chapter 3):

- Gender
- Monthly income
- Educational background
- Location
- Other apps they use
- Smartphone habits
- Devices they use

Important   If you don't know anything about your target group, check mobile-platform-specific numbers of operating systems and hardware specifications. Furthermore, analyze and gather information about apps that are similar to yours. This is a good starting point to help you gather potential user information.

Based on the requirements and features of your app and knowledge of your target group, you can ask specific questions to collect information for your testing work and scope:

- Is it important to find critical bugs quickly?
- Should the app be tested only in common user scenarios?
- On which mobile platforms should testing be performed?
- What are our customers' carrier networks?
- Are there any areas within the app that are likely to change on a regular basis?
- Is the release (submission) date of the app already known?
- Is there a roadmap for future releases?

Don't hesitate to ask these kinds of questions as they're important, and the answers will help you to define your next testing steps and priorities. Don't worry if you forget to ask a question before you start writing the test strategy— it's better to ask a question whenever it comes up than not at all.

In the next step you should collect information about the development environment within the company. It is important to know which tools are used to set up a development and test pipeline. Which continuous integration server is being used? Which tools are used to build the app? And which backend technologies are used to process the requests from the mobile app? You also need to know about the architecture of the production environment.

To go about collecting all of this information, you should ascertain the answers to the following questions:

- What kind of software development tools are already available and in use within the company?

- Is there a common build pipeline that must be used?

- Which continuous integration server is used for the project?

- Which tools are used to build the mobile app?

- Which technologies are used to process the mobile requests?

- What skills, such as programming languages, are available within the mobile team?

- How many mobile devices are available within the company for testing?

- What tools and technologies are used in the production environment?

- How many people do we expect to use the mobile app?

The answers to these questions will help you choose, for example, the test automation tool based on the technical knowledge within your team. They will help you to define the test levels and techniques, and furthermore they will provide a first overview of all technologies involved in the mobile project. Knowledge of the development, test, and production environment is very important when it comes to coordinating testing within the project.

> **Important**   Collecting requirements and features is important as you need such useful information for your mobile test strategy. This kind of information is a good starting point for planning your testing activities and will help you to define a testing scope.

Testing Scope

Once you've defined the requirements, you can specify the scope for your test strategy. It's not possible to test an app on every possible hardware and software combination. You should therefore reduce the scope of your testing efforts and initially concentrate on the important parts of the mobile app.

There are four ways to reduce your testing scope:

- Single-device scope
- Multidevice scope
- Maximum device scope
- Use-case scope

Single-Device Scope

The single-device scope focuses on one mobile device during testing. This approach can or will be used if only one device is to be supported by the app or if there is very little time available for the project. In the event of time pressure, you'll probably choose only the most popular device used by your targeted customers. This device will be used for testing with just one mobile carrier network and possibly a Wi-Fi connection. Another approach could be to choose a device from the device group that has older hardware specifications and could therefore cause more problems for the developers in terms of support. You're likely to find more bugs and problems, such as performance or other issues, with this device than with the latest device.

Using only the single-device scope can be dangerous for the mobile app, for the success of the project, or even for the whole company. It is very likely that you'll miss important bugs that occur on other devices and that your customers will submit bad ratings to the app stores. If the app supports only one device—for example, if it is an internal enterprise app—this approach can be used. On the other hand, it's better to test on only one device than to skip the entire testing process.

Multidevice Scope

As the name suggests, the multidevice scope focuses either on several devices from one mobile platform or on multiple mobile platforms. Select the platforms and test devices based on your target group, and then group the devices as described in Chapter 3 in the section "Mobile Device Groups." If you don't have any information about your target group, use the Internet to search for platform-specific numbers and statistics, which will help you select the mobile platform and devices to concentrate on.

A really nice Web page provided by Google is "Our Mobile Planet"[1] where you can get information based on the country, age, gender, user behavior, and behavior during the current year.

Maximum Device Scope

The maximum device scope focuses on as many mobile platforms and devices as possible. This approach can be used for mass-market apps intended to reach as many customers as possible all over the world with no restrictions in terms of platform, device, carrier network, or target group. Testing an app for the mass market is very difficult because there will almost always be a hardware and software combination that doesn't work well with your app, and it's nearly impossible to find this combination. In order to handle and reduce this risk, you need to find a way to test on as many devices as possible.

This approach requires lots of research to gather information and statistics about current device usage, mobile platforms, and operating system versions. It requires information about the different carrier networks and connection speeds from around the world, and so forth.

Once you've collected the required information, consider using a combination of in-house testing, cloud testing, and crowd testing to handle the mass-market situation. Bear in mind that testing just with in-house resources and devices will be either too limited in scope or too expensive.

Use-Case Scope

Besides choosing a hardware testing scope to downsize your testing work, you can also choose a use-case scope to limit the workload. With this approach you can concentrate on certain parts or features of the mobile app and leave out less important ones, such as help texts or edge cases. Nearly every project is under extreme time pressure, thus making it important to define which parts of the app must be included in the testing scope and which can be left out. Write down both parts in your test strategy and describe the use cases that have to be tested and why. If there is enough time, the less important parts should be tested as well.

You may want or need to include the following test scope information in your test strategy:

- Which approach should be used in the project?
- Is it possible to combine approaches for certain parts of the app?

---

1. http://think.withgoogle.com/mobileplanet/en/

- Why was this approach selected?
- What are the required and main use cases of the app?

Define Test Levels and Test Techniques

Once you've defined the requirements and scope, you need to think about the different test levels and test techniques you want to use in your project. Keep in mind the quality assurance measures overview from Chapter 4, "How to Test Mobile Apps" (the section "Traditional Testing"), when defining them. This overview will help you to derive the test levels and techniques for your mobile app.

Test Levels

As shown in Chapter 5, "Mobile Test Automation and Tools," the focus of test levels from non-mobile software development tends to shift throughout the mobile software development process. The "mobile test pyramid" shows that the unit testing level is the smallest part compared to end-to-end testing, beta testing, and manual testing.

In most software development projects, the developers are responsible for writing unit tests. This is also the case with mobile app projects. Mobile testers are responsible for writing the end-to-end test automation including integration testing. However, everyone on the team should be responsible for the app's quality—they should all support the mobile tester in his or her work.

As mentioned in several chapters in this book, manual testing is a very important part of a mobile development project and forms an essential part of the test levels in a mobile project. However, there are other levels that are important for manual testing: acceptance, alpha, and beta testing. User acceptance tests can be performed to test the mobile app against the user requirements to verify that the app covers them all. This step is usually carried out by a tester, product manager, or the customer.

In mobile development projects, alpha and beta testing are important test levels that should form part of your test strategy. Whenever a feature is implemented within your app, you should test it with potential customers to gather early feedback about it. If testing with potential customers is not possible within alpha tests, you could try testing the feature with your work colleagues to get feedback from outside of the development team.

Once the mobile app has reached a defined maturity—for example, all of the features have been implemented or only two bugs were found in the last week—you should consider using beta distribution tools or a crowd-based testing approach to perform beta tests with potential customers. The criteria that determine that a testing phase is finished and that the next one is ready for execution also need to be documented in the test strategy.

Typical software test levels that should be used in a mobile development project are listed here:

- Automated testing
  - Unit testing
  - End-to-end testing (including integration testing)
- Manual testing
  - Acceptance testing
  - Alpha testing
  - Beta testing
- Regression testing

Once you've defined the test levels, you should also consider defining how intensively each level should be tested from a functional and nonfunctional point of view. Please keep in mind that not all test types will be included at every test level.

Furthermore, it can be helpful to define some metrics that measure the current state of the application. Possible metrics may include the following:

- Each feature must have at least one unit test.
- Each feature must have at least one end-to-end test.
- There should be no warnings or errors in the static analysis check.

Functional testing should include the following:

- Identify the functionality of the mobile app.
- Test the different parts against the functional requirements.
- Define and execute the test cases.
- Create input data based on the specifications.
- Compare the actual and the expected outputs.

Nonfunctional testing should include the following points:

- Load testing
- Performance testing

- Usability testing
- Security testing
- Portability testing
- Accessibility testing
- Internationalization/localization testing

The following test-level information could be used in your test strategy:

- Which test levels will be used in the project and why?
- Which parts are to be used for functional and nonfunctional testing?
- Define and describe the automated test levels. Which parts need to be unit tested and which parts will be tested using an end-to-end test automation tool?
- Define and describe when the software has reached a certain maturity and can be used for alpha and beta testing.
- Define and describe metrics relevant to the project.

Test Techniques

You can draw upon quality assurance measures (Chapter 4) to define your test techniques and methods. Consider using static and dynamic approaches to test your mobile app from different points of view.

As described in Chapter 4, I recommend using static code analysis tools in your static testing approach to test your mobile app's code for any bugs or problems. Keep in mind that the app code is not executed during static testing. Furthermore, all of the project documentation should be reviewed for completeness.

With the dynamic testing approach you should use white and black box testing techniques to test your app. White box testing should be done by the developers and covers the following:

- Statement coverage
- Path coverage
- Branch coverage
- Decision coverage
- Control flow testing
- Data flow testing

Black box testing should be done by the software testers including:

- Equivalence classes
- Boundary value analysis
- Decision tables
- State transitions
- Cause-effect graph

However, the developers should also test for boundary values and state transitions at the unit testing level in order to be sure that each unit correctly handles those situations.

Your test strategy should also include a written record of which test technique is to be handled by whom.

Besides the aforementioned techniques, you should consider using exploratory and risk-based testing to organize and downsize the testing work within your mobile team.

> **Important**   Define test levels for your mobile app based on its features and requirements. Quality assurance measures will help you define your test methods and techniques.

The following information about test techniques could form part of your test strategy:

- Which test technique will be used with your project and why?
- Define and describe the order of the test techniques; for example, static code analysis and document review are to be followed by white box testing, black box testing, and then exploratory test sessions involving the whole team.
- Which team members are to apply the different test techniques?
- Define and describe the manual testing process, such as acceptance testing, exploratory testing, alpha and beta testing.
- Define and describe the test exit criteria for white and black box testing, for example, 80% branch coverage with white box testing.

Test Data

Nearly every app processes, creates, and sends data from the mobile app via data networks to different backend systems. The processed and transferred data differs from mobile app to mobile app and has differing requirements and complexities. One component of your mobile test strategy should be the required test data. It is important to define the test data as realistically as possible based on the features and requirements of your app.

The following three points are an example of different test data types:

- **Configuration data:** This data includes configurations for the mobile app or for the backend system. It could, for example, include decision rules for rules engines and/or settings for databases and firewalls.

- **Stable data:** This usually involves data with a low rate of change and a long duration. A typical example of this is customer information such as username and password, or product information.

- **Temporary data:** This kind of data is likely to change frequently, meaning that it can be used only once or will be created while the app is running, for example, payment details or vouchers.

Once the test data requirements are clear, find a way to save the test data so you can re-create and reset the data in a defined state whenever you need it. One possible solution for this is a database where the stored information can be used during the development and testing process. Another advantage of this is that you can also use the database for manual and automated testing. On the other hand, you can use test data management tools to organize data within your project.

Once you've set up the reset and re-creation process, you should start creating the data as soon as possible as this will help you and your colleagues during the app development process.

Depending on the app, you may need lots of test data. If this is the case, it might be a good idea to use a generator to create the data automatically. If a data generator is used, it is important that the functionality and necessary parameters be documented.

If test data is available within your project, don't forget to adapt it to new features and changes. It is very likely that over time features will be improved and the test data requirements will change. Your test strategy should therefore also outline a process for updating the test data, including responsibilities and triggers for the update process. It is also recommended that you define a strategy for how outdated test data should be archived in order to reproduce incoming bugs in old features or versions of your app.

The following test data information could form part of your test strategy:

- How is the test data generated?
- Where is the test data stored?

- How is the documentation handled, for example, test data together with test results?
- How often will the test data be updated?
- Who is responsible for the test data?

Select Target Devices and Test Environment

Now that you've described the features, requirements, test level, and technique as well as the test data, you need to think about the test environment and test target devices for your strategy. As you learned in Chapter 3, grouping your test devices or mobile Web browsers is a good approach to determine which devices should be used for the mobile app. Creating such mobile device groups requires information about your target customer group and their usage scenarios. Don't forget the testing scopes described in this chapter when doing so.

Once the device groups are in place, you'll need to select devices from those groups to have them available within your team. It is recommended that you have at least one device from each group available for testing. However, I recommend at least five devices from each group in order to have a broader mix of hardware and software combinations with different form factors and displays. You should also keep a record of why you chose those test devices.

Now that you know which devices are needed for testing, you need to buy or rent them. Buying all of the devices you need can be expensive and perhaps is not an option due to the project's budget. A good approach to save some money is online auctions where you can buy used devices. In most cases the devices are in good enough shape for your testing work.

If buying is not an option at all, you can rent the devices. As mentioned in Chapter 3, there are several mobile device lab providers on the market that will lend you the devices you need for a set period. However, check the rental prices and compare them with the device price. If you want to rent the devices for a prolonged period, renting will probably be more expensive than buying the device in the first place.

Another alternative is Open Device Labs[2] where the devices can be borrowed for free. Check the Open Device Labs map to find one in your area. If you want a free device, you can also ask around at your company or even see if someone in your family has the device you need that you can borrow for a while.

Once you've specified your device strategy, you need to think about the test environment: the backend systems. You need to know the architecture of the backend systems such as databases, payment systems, APIs, and any other kind of system involved in the mobile project. If you have systems information, you

---

2. http://opendevicelab.com/

need to be sure that it's also available within the test environment so you can test as though you're in the production environment. If your test strategy contains in-the-wild or on-the-move tests, there's an additional requirement: the test environment must be accessible from outside the company network.

The following information about the target devices and the test environment could form part of your test strategy:

- Which devices will be used for testing?
- Why are those devices used for testing?
- Are the devices available within the company or do you need to acquire them?
- What are your reasons for choosing those test devices?
- What are the requirements for the test devices and the test environment?
- Is there an update policy for the mobile devices?
- When will new devices be integrated into the development and testing process?
- What are the usage scenarios of the system?
- What does the backend system consist of?
- Is the test environment similar to the live environment?
- Can the test environment be used for testing purposes from outside the company network?

Manual and in-the-Wild Testing

As you have learned so far, mobile testing requires lots of manual testing and testing in real-life environments. Think of the example with the ski and snowboard app from Chapter 1, "What's Special about Mobile Testing?," where testing on a mountain is required to see if the mobile app actually works under real conditions.

Manual testing in the wild is essential for your mobile app and requires lots of planning beforehand to avoid useless test scenarios while testing on the move. You should therefore try to identify common real-world usage scenarios for your mobile app and its features. Write the scenarios down in your test strategy and rank them based on priority and importance to your project.

Furthermore, it is recommended that you define test routes, such as by bus, train, car, plane, or while walking. Within these routes, describe possible scenarios that should be tested. These routes allow you to simulate real mobile users while they commute to work or while they're traveling around.

Last but not least, you should define data network scenarios based on your target group. After gathering information about your target group, you will know in which regions they live and what kind of data networks and speeds are available, for example, 4G, 3G, or EDGE. Based on that information, you can limit app testing to those network speeds, but don't forget to test on different network providers.

Here are a few example usage scenarios:

- Test your app based on its features, such as outside in sunny places or inside an office.
- Test to see if the app can be used in different weather conditions.
- Use multiple apps such as e-mail, chat, and news while your app is running in the background. Check to see if the app is influenced by other apps.

Here are some examples of route scenarios:

- Use the app while commuting to work by train, bus, or car.
- Use the app while running and check the behavior of the sensors.
- Use the app while walking through a city or the countryside and check the sensors and the GPS or compass.

Here are some examples of data network scenarios:

- Test how the app works in fast data networks like 4G or 3G.
- Test how the app handles the data network change from 4G to 3G or even 2G.
- Test how the app handles packet loss or a complete loss of network.

In-the-wild testing requires lots of movement and is a challenging task that needs to be handled during the app's development process. If you don't have the time or option to test your app in real-world scenarios, think about using crowd testing in tandem with your in-house testing work. However, remember the pros and cons of crowd testing from Chapter 6, "Additional Mobile Testing Methods," as they can have an impact on your project planning, coordination, timing, and budget.

Don't write complex test cases and scenarios with exact steps for in-the-wild testing. While you're on the move, you're unlikely to have a laptop with you to check the test cases. This is inefficient because it will destroy the real-life testing scenarios, behavior, and user simulation. You'll probably have a bag with you containing lots of devices for your in-the-wild testing. When planning such scenarios, keep them short and informative so that they can be used while on the move. I recommend that you print out the scenarios or write them down on a piece of paper so you can just read them and keep them in mind.

The following information about in-the-wild testing could form part of your test strategy:

- Define and describe the usage scenarios of your customers.

- Define and describe the test scenarios in the wild.

- Define and describe the different data networks that need to be used for testing.

Mobile Checklists and Tours

You can add mobile checklists and mobile tours to your mobile test strategy. As described in Chapter 4, mobile checklists can be very important for your mobile app as they help you keep a record of things that can't be automated or are likely to change on a frequent basis. If you know the requirements and features of your app, you'll probably also know the parts of the app that need to be tested repeatedly. In that case it's good to add those features to a checklist as part of your test strategy.

Based on the features of your app, it's useful to define mobile testing tours to concentrate your testing efforts on special parts of your app. Cem Kaner[3] describes a tour as ". . . an exploration of a product that is organized around a theme."

Using tours in your mobile testing work helps you to explore and understand how the mobile app works. It also helps you come up with new test ideas while you're testing the app. Please refer back to Chapter 4 for a description of some tours backed up with mnemonics.

Here are some examples of testing tours:

- **Feature tour:** Explore and test all of the possible features within the app.

- **Configuration tour:** Explore and test every part of the app that can be configured.

- **Gesture tour:** Use every possible gesture on every screen to see how the app handles the different inputs.

- **Orientation tour:** Change the orientation of every screen from portrait to landscape and vice versa to see if any problems arise.

---

3. http://kaner.com/?p=96

I use the following mobile mnemonics in my projects:

- FCC CUTS VIDS (http://michaeldkelly.com/blog/2005/9/20/touring-heuristic.html) from Michael Kelly
- I SLICED UP FUN (www.kohl.ca/articles/ISLICEDUPFUN.pdf) from Jonathan Kohl

The following information about mobile checklists and tours could form part of your test strategy:

- Which checklists will be used in the project and why?
- Describe the used checklists and tours.
- Describe when the checklists and tours should be used and by whom.

Test Automation

Test automation can also form part of a mobile test strategy. Depending on the mobile app and its lifecycle, you may not need to automate it. If that's the case, it's important that you document and describe the reasons why test automation is not necessary.

However, if your app requires test automation, you should start to think about automation and the tools you want to use as soon as possible. Think back to the different mobile test automation concepts in Chapter 5 and their pros and cons. Choose the tool that best fits your current project situation and where you have already gained some experience with one of the tools or programming skills, or where you have a mobile testing setup or environment in place. This will save you lots of time and money.

Describe the mobile test automation tool in your test strategy and why you chose it for this project. Based on the described features and requirements, you can define the parts of the app that should be automated and which do not need to be.

During the next step you should describe the devices on which the automated test has to run and in what environment the tests should be executed.

Your mobile app project should find the right balance between real devices and virtual devices if you're not able to test everything on real devices. A mixture of real and virtual devices can also be more cost-effective.

Once you've defined the devices and test automation environment, I recommend that you also define test suites to group the different automated test cases based on common features, areas, and requirements within your app. With the help of the test suites you can decide which tests should be executed when and how often. For example, you can define a smoke test suite containing several automated tests from each part of the app to make sure a commit to the central code repository didn't break anything. This test suite should be small and run every time the code changes in order to receive fast feedback and to swiftly inform the developers of any problems.

Here are some examples of test suites:

- Smoke test suite containing a few test scripts to check the basic functions of the app and to provide fast feedback

- Medium test suite or a test suite containing only specific functionality

- Full regression test suite containing all test scripts to be executed once a day or during the night

- Test suites containing only user scenarios such as the registration or checkout process

Test suites can be a great way to create a balance between fast feedback and broad test coverage.

When the test suites are in place, define when they should be executed; for example, the smoke test suite must be run after every commit by the developer. The medium test suite could be executed every two hours. The full regression test suite should be executed once every night.

You should also define where the test automation should be executed. One such solution can be where the unit tests are executed on the developer's local environment before changes are pushed to the central repository. The unit tests and end-to-end tests can be executed on the CI server.

The following information about test automation could form part of your test strategy:

- Is a CI server used for the build process?

- Which CI server is used and why?

- Which test environment is used to execute the test automation?

- Which test automation tools are used in the project?

- Are the tests executed on real devices and virtual devices?

- Which devices must be connected to the CI server and why?

- Is a cloud provider used for the test automation?

- Define and describe the test suites and groups.

- Define and describe the different build triggers and execution times.

- Define and describe where the different test automation suites will be executed, for example, everything on a local developer machine or only on the CI server.

Product Risks

Every project is exposed to different kinds of risk. It is important to work out both project and feature risks so you can then define possible solutions for them. Consider both the likelihood of risk occurrence and risk impact. If the product risks are clear, you can start implementing a risk analysis approach that can be used by the whole team when defining, implementing, and testing new features.

The following information about the product risks could form part of your test strategy:

- Which parts are critical to the business?
- What is the likelihood of the product risks occurring?
- How should the business-critical parts be tested?
- What is the potential impact if a critical problem occurs?
- How is the feature risk analysis performed?
- Is there a disaster plan in place?

> **Important**   Creating a mobile test strategy is not easy as it needs to cover lots of mobile testing information. Your strategy may also need to be modified during the development process because of changed product features or priorities.

Mobile Launch Strategy

As important as the mobile test strategy is, it's also really important to write down a mobile launch strategy. Launching an app is not easy, and lots of problems can occur during and after it has been launched. This part of the chapter will describe the important pre- and post-launch activities for a mobile app.

Pre-Launch—Check the Release Material

As mentioned in Chapter 4, you should think about putting together a release checklist to make sure that all the release information is available and in place. You should also perform the update and installation test before submitting the app to the app store.

The tests you perform before committing the app to the app store shouldn't be limited to the app itself. Your launch strategy should outline if and how the backend services are tested before a new release.

Ask yourself the question "Does the new version of the app require some new backend services or API calls?" If so, are those services or API calls already live in the backend system? If not, it's very likely that your app will be rejected by the app store vendor. If backend services are available, check the new and existing features of the app in the production environment one final time.

When the app is ready for launch, check the release notes and feature description in the new app store information material. Read through the texts and compare them with the new and existing features. In the release notes it's important to be specific about the new features; describe them well and explain them to the users. It is also important to provide the release notes and app description in every supported language.

Don't forget to check the screenshots of the app. They should be in the same language as the notes, be the same size as the previous screenshots, and have the same status bar icons showing the time, battery, and network state. Figure 7.1 and Figure 7.2 provide examples of what not to do: the status bar contains different icons for the same app.

The app store screenshots need to have the same status bar and the same look-and-feel in order to portray a professional image.

If the new features are described by means of a video, watch the video again and listen to the feature description and information it provides. Ask if there is more marketing material available that needs to be checked.

Last but not least, there is one really important point: don't release your app to your customers on a Friday evening or just before you leave the office. In most of the app stores it takes some time (up to several hours) before your app is listed and available for download. If the office is empty, no one can react to any critical bugs or release problems that may occur right after the release.

Some app stores don't have an app submission process and can therefore react quickly to problems by releasing a hot-fix version of your app right after

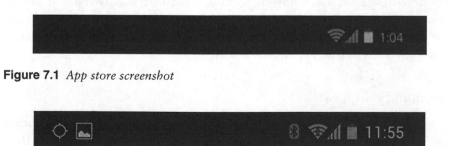

Figure 7.1 *App store screenshot*

Figure 7.2 *App store screenshot of the same app with different status bar information and sizes*

the last release. When possible, release your app either in the morning or on the weekend so that you have some time to react to critical issues.

The following information about the release material could form part of your launch strategy:

- Define and use a release checklist.

- Perform the update and installation test again.

- Check to make sure all of the backend services and APIs are available on the production environment.

- Define which new and old features should be checked again on the live environment.

- Define and describe how the app store material, including release notes, screenshots, and videos, should be checked.

- Define and describe when the app should be submitted to the app store.

Post-Release—What Happens after an App Launch?

The post-release phase starts once you've released your mobile app. During this phase you and your team should pay attention to several points to get feedback from your customers and to handle any questions or problems they send you.

The first thing you should do right after releasing your app is to download it and install it from the app store to make sure it's working as expected. If the version is OK, you should archive it on a file server to be able to install it again later, for example, to reproduce problems or bugs that may be reported. This step can also be handled by your build pipeline within the continuous integration system.

However, there are a few more issues that you, your team, and your company need to handle. The following sections describe the activities that can be performed after releasing your app in order to get further information about your customers and any potential problems. It is important to define and write down such items in your app launch strategy.

Community Support

Providing community or customer support for a released product is essential, especially if you're offering a paid app. Whenever users have a problem, they should be able to contact someone at your company or the mobile team to get answers to their questions or problems. If no one looks after the users or communities, they will write bad reviews or simply stop using your app.

You should therefore make sure you man every possible social media channel and check for customer feedback, questions, or problems that need to be looked into. It is important to respond to such queries to give customers the feeling that someone is listening to them. It is also possible to select some users and ask them questions about the new version of the app. The gathered feedback can then be used to improve the app in future releases.

> **Important**   If your company has a customer support department, I recommend that you spend a bit of time with them to get a feeling for customer needs and problems.

Reviews

The next channel you have to monitor after releasing your app is the app store reviews. Read them carefully to get some feedback and bug reports from your users. However, I highly recommend that you handle those reviews with care. There are lots of people out there who like to write negative feedback about apps that is not true. Whenever a user complains about your app, try to reproduce the problem in order to be able to create a bug report aimed at fixing the issue in a subsequent release. If you're not able to reproduce the issue, try to reply to the reviewer to ask specific questions in order to get more information.

However, not all app stores provide a reply function within their review section so that you can talk to your customers. If the app store doesn't provide such a feature, you can write your own review, stating that you are the developer, tester, or product manager of the app and would like further information or are offering some sort of solution to the problem. However, be sure you're allowed to write reviews within the app store to reply to previous reviews. Please refer to the app store review guidelines to make sure you're not violating any rules. If you're able to reply to reviews, use this functionality to interact with your customers and to learn from them.

If you get lots of negative feedback due to a misunderstanding within the app or its features, you can also provide some sort of troubleshooting guide or tutorial within the app description. However, if you get lots of negative feedback about your app because the customers didn't understand the feature, you need to rethink the whole app or feature, perform additional usability testing, and provide an update as soon as possible.

Crash Reports

Another valuable source of information is the crash reports of your app. If you implemented tools like HockeyApp,[4] crashlytics,[5] or TestFlight,[6] you should check them after the release to see if there are any problems with your app. Not every problem that occurs during runtime will end up being an app crash. If your app has good exception handling in place, errors will not be shown to the user but will be captured by the crash reporting tools. This kind of information is very important to help you improve the app in further releases.

The tools provide a Web interface where the top app crashes are ranked, grouped, and categorized. They show the total number of crashes and the number of users affected by these problems. Nearly every crash reporting tool provides nice graphs showing, for example, app distribution and app crashes over time. Some of the crash reporting tools provide an option to send feedback from within the app to the crash reporting backend. Furthermore, some of the tools offer third-party integration for a bug tracking system.

If you haven't implemented a crash reporting tool, some app store manufacturers provide basic crash reporting functionality that can be used as a starting point.

> **Important**   Implement a crash reporting tool as it will help you and your team to get more insight into the problems and crashes within your app.

Tracking and Statistics

To gather information about your customers and their usage of your app, you should implement some sort of tracking mechanism to collect important data. This kind of information will be aggregated by tracking tools to generate statistics about your app and feature usage. If your app uses a tracking mechanism, check the statistics generated post-release.

Depending on the tracking implementation, you can get information such as:

• Mobile operating system version

• Mobile device manufacturer

• Device model

• Display size

---

4. http://hockeyapp.net/features/
5. http://try.crashlytics.com/
6. www.testflightapp.com

- Mobile browser version
- Number of page views
- How often a certain feature was used
- How often the registration process was aborted

With the help of those statistics and numbers, try to understand your users' behavior so you can tweak the app and its features. The following list is a sampling of some mobile tracking tools:

- adjust (www.adjust.com/)
- appsfire (http://appsfire.com/)
- AppsFlyer (www.appsflyer.com/)
- Clicktale (www.clicktale.com/)
- iMobiTrax (www.imobitrax.com/)
- MobileAppTracking (www.mobileapptracking.com/)

As you can see, it's not easy to create mobile test and launch strategies as both require and contain lots of information about testing topics and pre- and post-launch activities. Please keep in mind that such strategies are not set in stone. You should rework and adapt both strategies whenever changes occur in terms of the product, risks, or any other priorities. Mobile test and launch strategy documents are an ongoing process, and every team member should be responsible for updating and extending them.

Summary

The main topic of Chapter 7 was the mobile test and launch strategies. Every mobile team needs test and launch strategies in order to remember important tasks before and after the release of the app.

When establishing a mobile test strategy, the following topics should be covered and defined:

- Requirements definition
- Testing scope
- Test levels
- Test techniques
- Test data

- Target devices and environment
- Test automation

With the questions provided in this part of the chapter you are now able to set up your own mobile test strategy for your app or for your company.

The other part of this chapter covered the mobile launch strategy. The importance of the release material, including feature descriptions, screenshots, and any other marketing material, was described. With the help of the questions provided, you should find it very easy to check whether everything is available for the release.

After the release of the app it is important to have community support in place, where users can ask questions when they have any kind of problem with your app. Furthermore, the importance of crash reports, tracking, and user statistics was established.

Chapter 8

Important Skills
for Mobile Testers

Software testers and mobile testers in particular are facing more and more requirements as mobile apps are becoming increasingly complex and the time to market is getting shorter. Mobile testers need to be able to efficiently test complex mobile applications within a very short period of time to deliver excellent products to customers. Besides testing knowledge, mobile testers must have several other important skills to manage the complexity of the systems and the huge number of different scenarios.

This chapter is all about software testing skills and how to improve your mobile testing skills to become a better mobile tester.

Skill Set of a Mobile Tester

Besides knowledge and skills regarding software testing methods, approaches, mobile apps, and devices, testers must have a solid basic set of soft skills if they want to be successful in the mobile development business. In the following sections of this chapter you'll read about various skills every software tester should have.

Communication

The ability to communicate is one of the most important skills a software tester must have. Software testers must be able to describe their testing work to different kinds of people at different levels within the company. They need to be able to talk to developers, designers, product managers, project managers, other software testers, and management as well as to customers. Talking to other software testers and developers requires technical skills and detailed knowledge of the different parts of the software. Reporting bugs and showing others their mistakes can quickly lead to negative emotions, which is why it's important to report bugs in a clear and concise way without bringing emotions into the conversation.

Talking to product managers, project managers, designers, or management requires the ability to describe problems and bugs to nontechnicians at a higher level in a way that is clear and understandable.

In addition to verbal communication, software testers need strong written communication skills as they have to be able to describe problems and bugs in such a way that every potential stakeholder can understand them.

Listening is also an essential part of communication, and software testers must be able to listen carefully when other people are talking and describing their thoughts or problems. It is important that you don't interrupt other people when they're talking. If you have any questions, make a note of them and ask them once the person has finished.

To help you improve your communication skills, I recommend that you read, read, and read—not just books but blogs, newspapers, and any other kind of material that will help you improve and expand your vocabulary, especially if you're not communicating in your native language.

I also recommend that you watch movies or TV series in other languages to bolster your vocabulary. If you have more time available and want to spend some money, you can attend language and communication classes, which are a great way to improve your language and communication skills.

Last but not least, I recommend that you give talks at user groups, conferences, or within your company. Such experience will have a major impact on your communication skills because you get feedback from your audience right away.

Poor communication generally leads to disagreement and misunderstandings, which can be avoided by following some simple rules:

- Listen carefully.
- Don't interrupt other people while they're speaking.
- Don't speak too loudly.
- Don't speak too quickly.
- Speak clearly and precisely.
- Make eye contact with your audience.
- Don't get personal when communicating with other people.

- Be able to communicate on different levels, ranging from technical to non-technical audiences.

- Improve your vocabulary by reading books, blogs, and newspapers.

> **Important** Software testers need to be diplomats, technicians, and politicians all rolled into one as they have to be able to talk and listen to different stakeholders within the company.

Curiosity

It's human nature to be curious, and software testers need to be curious to explore, discover, and learn new things about the software they're testing and the product domain. A curious software tester explores the software to get as much information as possible out of the system to identify potential problems and raise interesting questions about the product. It's important to go beyond the usual software testing approaches and methods to discover new things.

To be able to discover new things, it's important to be open to new technologies and willing to try new approaches and methods. A curious software tester doesn't rely on statements from other people; he or she questions them to gain more information.

If you'd like to train your curiosity, I recommend that you download a random mobile app or software application and start exploring its features. Try new approaches and methods while you're exploring the software. Try to break the system and start questioning the features. Make note of everything that feels wrong or evokes some sort of strange reaction during your exploration so you can raise questions or point out any possible problems with the software.

> **Important** Be curious; explore and discover every part of the software to raise problems or questions. Don't rely on statements from other people; question them.

Critical Thinking

Another really important skill every software tester must have is critical thinking. With the help of critical thinking good software testers are able to see the larger context of the software and its features. They are also able to break down the software or the requirements through analysis and reflection. This is very important to gain a deep understanding of the product and to focus on the right testing work.

The following quote from Michael Bolton describes critical thinking in a nice way: "Critical thinking is thinking about thinking with the aim of not getting fooled."[1]

It's important to question your own thinking, testing methods, and approaches as well as your own decisions and the software that needs to be tested. Ask yourself the following questions:

- What is the problem of this feature/software?
- Is it really a problem?
- Why have you tested this feature that way?
- Have you thought about this?
- Are you sure about this?

A very good three-word critical thinking heuristic from James Bach[2] is Huh? Really? So? Each word suggests an investigation pattern that indicates assumptions, sloppy inferences, and misunderstandings:

- **Huh?**
  - Do you understand what others are talking about?
  - Is it confusing?
  - Is it vague?
- **Really?**
  - Is it factually true?
  - What evidence do we have for it?
- **So?**
  - Why does this matter?
  - To whom does it matter?
  - How much does it matter?

Use this critical thinking heuristic in your project and start questioning your own work and the mobile app. For further information about critical thinking, take a look at the slides from Michael Bolton's course, Critical Thinking for Testers.[3]

---

1. www.developsense.com/presentations/2010-04-QuestioningBestPracticeMyths.pdf
2. www.satisfice.com/
3. www.developsense.com/presentations/2012-11-EuroSTAR-CriticalThinkingForTesters.pdf

Tenacity

Reporting bugs or raising issues can be exhausting and difficult. Not every issue found by a software tester will be fixed. The issue may not be important enough for other team members, or perhaps there is not enough time to fix it. It is part of the software tester's job to be tenacious and fight to get bugs resolved. If the software tester thinks a bug may be critical for the customers or the system, he or she needs to initiate a discussion to describe and explain why it needs to be fixed in the next release. The keywords here are "Bug Advocacy." The Association for Software Testing provides a training course on this important topic.[4] If you want to get a first impression of Bug Advocacy, take a look at the slides from Cem Kaner.[5]

High stress levels are common before a release and often cause developers or project managers to neglect the agreed-upon software quality standards. In such situations software testers must be tenacious and explain or raise bugs over and over again until the software quality standards have been met. But be careful with this as you may end up being considered a nuisance. Here it's important to rely on your strong communication skills.

Software testers have to be tenacious while testing software such as mobile apps. Depending on the kind of app being tested, such as a game, it is very likely that certain game levels have to be tested over and over again in order to be sure that each level works as expected. This can also be very exhausting but requires tenacity or some test automation.

> **Important**   Be tenacious during testing and during possible discussions about bugs and errors within the application.

Constant Learner

The current mobile world and technology are changing rapidly. To maintain pace with this environment, software testers and, in particular, mobile testers must be able to adapt and learn new things really quickly. Software testers need to take note of changes taking place around them in order to adapt and learn new approaches, methods, and technologies.

To keep pace and learn new techniques and tools, software testers can read blogs or books and attend conferences and training courses. On the other hand, it's important that software testers be able to learn during their daily job, while testing software, and while using tools such as test automation tools. Whenever

---

4. www.associationforsoftwaretesting.org/training/courses/bug-advocacy/
5. www.kaner.com/pdfs/BugAdvocacy.pdf

a new tool, technique, or technology enters the market, every software tester should be motivated to gather information about these new items and to learn about them.

> **Important**   Learning and improving personal skills should be a lifelong habit.

Creativity

Another important skill a software tester should have is creativity. It is important to be able to generate creative ideas to test software in very different ways so as to find more bugs and provide the team with useful information. The creativity process starts with designing the test cases and test data. Software testers need to think in different ways to find every conceivable use for a piece of software.

When the default testing approach is complete and there's some project time left for testing activities, I recommend that you test the software again from a completely different point of view; for example, walk through the bugs again to generate new testing ideas, or talk to colleagues or beta testers to get new ideas for your testing work. Try to be creative with your data inputs, when using the navigation, or anything else that comes to mind. You'll be surprised about the results from that kind of testing and will no doubt come across some more bugs.

> **Important**   Mobile testers in particular have to be creative in order to use mobile devices in different ways by paying attention to all the interfaces, sensors, and locations.

Customer Focus

Every software tester should have a strong customer focus. It's important that software testers try to think like a customer in order to determine whether the software being tested meets customer needs. Testers therefore need to have lots of passion and determination and be able to identify strongly with customers.

A strong customer focus requires you to be a product and field expert within your team. You also need to have an overview of released features and functionality and be able to keep an eye out for future releases. It is very important to be aware of customer behavior in order to know which features and functionality they use. If possible, software testers should talk to customers to determine their needs and problems. This can be a challenging job, so software testers have to be patient.

When software testers have a strong customer focus, they can contribute their knowledge to every phase of the software development process, which in turn helps to build better products. To help improve customer focus, I recommend spending a couple of weeks working with your customer support department to get a better feeling for customer needs.

Programming and Technical Skills

The fact that software products and mobile apps are becoming increasingly complex leads to the challenge that mobile testers also need to have solid programming skills as they help software testers to understand the system under test, to communicate with developers at code level, to review code from developers or other software testers, and to write test automation code which is now becoming essential in every project.

Mobile testers with no programming skills need to train themselves by reading a book about programming languages or patterns, by following a programming tutorial on the Internet, or by attending a programming course. It's also possible to ask a developer if he or she can train the mobile tester within a project or company.

Thanks to programming skills, mobile testers are able to write test automation code from unit to end-to-end level. They are able to attend code reviews to ask technical questions and are likely able to write shell scripts in order to automate either a build pipeline or any other task that the team needs to perform.

Besides coding skills, every mobile tester must be able to understand technical system architectures in order to be able to ask critical questions about the architecture and to know how to test every part of it.

> **Important**   Every mobile tester needs programming skills in order to be able to write test automation code and to be able to attend code reviews and technical discussions.

How to Improve Your Mobile Testing Skills

As mentioned in several parts of this book, the mobile world is changing rapidly, so you'll need to hone your skills every day to keep pace with the mobile testing world. You have to constantly learn new things to generate new testing ideas, to collaborate with developers during their work with programming skills, and you'll also need to understand customer needs.

In order to improve your mobile testing skills it is important to have at least one mobile device available. In most cases this is your private and personal device. If possible, I recommend that you have several devices available at home with different mobile platforms so you can learn everything about those platforms. You don't need to keep buying the latest devices; you can settle for used phones or even older versions to learn about each platform. If you're not in a position to buy lots of devices, keep in mind the Open Device Labs, where you're able to borrow different devices for free.

Learn from Other Apps

A very easy way to improve your mobile testing skills is to learn from other apps. I recommend installing and using as many apps as possible from different categories within different app stores to see how they work and behave. Check how other apps have implemented their navigation and update mechanism and how they use mobile-specific features such as the camera or other sensors.

However, besides using them, it's important to check the update texts of those apps. I recommend that you uncheck the automatic update functionality of all of your apps so you can install new versions manually. Before pressing the update button in the different mobile app stores, read the update texts and app descriptions carefully. There are lots of companies or developers who are really precise when describing what the new version of the app is all about. They describe which bugs are fixed with the new version and which new features have been added.

If there is a bug description in an app's update text, try to reproduce the bug so you can see it with your own eyes. This can be a lot of fun, but you may find it takes a while to provoke the bug. But this is in itself a great way to learn lots of new things.

You will probably get new testing ideas, come across new ways to use an app and new approaches to provoking a bug, and learn things that you may never have thought about before. The following sections will provide some examples involving different kinds of bugs and descriptions from mobile apps I check from time to time.

> **Important** The app screenshots in the "Crashes on Specific Devices" section are anonymized. All of the examples are based on the Google Play store. However, the same sort of bug and feature description can be found in every other mobile app store.

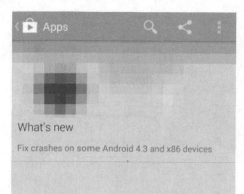

Figure 8.1 *App crashes on Android 4.3 and x86 devices*

Crashes on Specific Devices

The app in Figure 8.1 crashed when using Android version 4.3 and on some x86 devices. If you want to reproduce this crash, you'll need to get a device with Android 4.3. If such a device is available, find the section or app view that's crashing. This may prove to be rather difficult as there are lots of devices with Android 4.3 available and every device can behave differently. If you manage to find the crash, try to understand why it happened. Maybe it's due to a poor Internet connection or just a bad implementation.

Nevertheless, as shown in Figure 8.2, some apps have problems only with a certain version on the Android platform, so testing on several mobile operating systems is very important.

Keyboards

As I mentioned in Chapter 3, "Challenges in Mobile Testing," users are able to replace system apps such as the keyboard app with a third-party solution. This can lead to various problems as shown in Figure 8.3, which contains a bug report. To reproduce this issue, you need to install the third-party keyboard and start hunting the bug.

Widgets

Some mobile platforms support the use of widgets. When providing a widget, be sure that it won't freeze, crash, or consume too much battery power as shown in Figure 8.4.

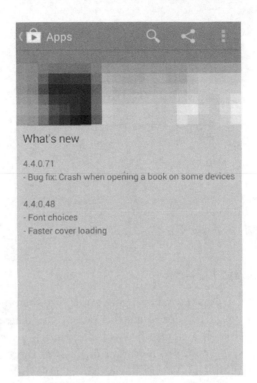

Figure 8.2 *App crashes on some devices*

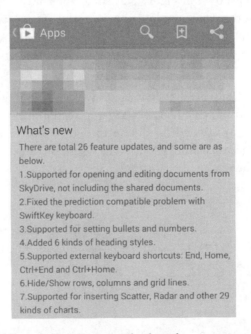

Figure 8.3 *App problems due to alternative keyboards*

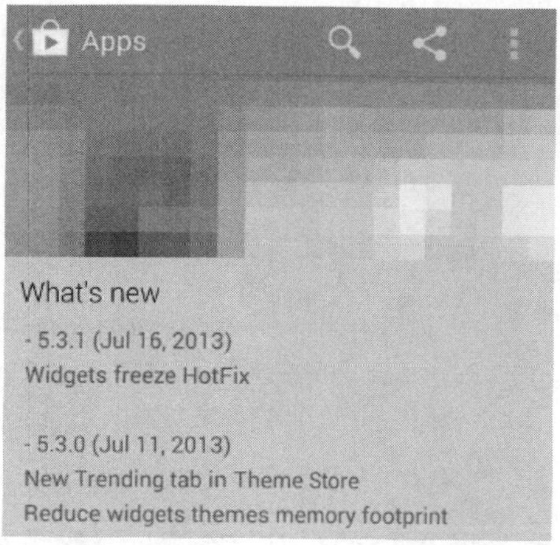

Apps

What's new

- 5.3.1 (Jul 16, 2013)
Widgets freeze HotFix

- 5.3.0 (Jul 11, 2013)
New Trending tab in Theme Store
Reduce widgets themes memory footprint

Figure 8.4 *Widget consumes too much battery power and freezes.*

Performance

As I have mentioned in several parts of this book, the loading time and performance of an app are essential to a successful app. The app description in Figure 8.5 provides some information about possible performance issues on the statistics page. To reproduce the performance issue of this app you need to get

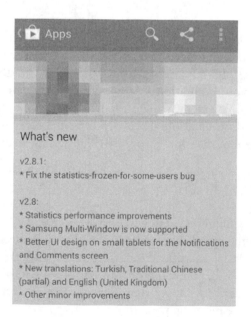

Apps

What's new

v2.8.1:
* Fix the statistics-frozen-for-some-users bug

v2.8:
* Statistics performance improvements
* Samsung Multi-Window is now supported
* Better UI design on small tablets for the Notifications
and Comments screen
* New translations: Turkish, Traditional Chinese
(partial) and English (United Kingdom)
* Other minor improvements

Figure 8.5 *Performance issues in some sections of the app*

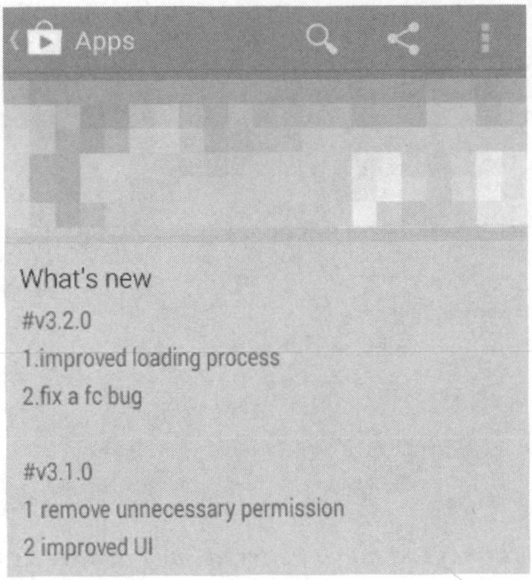

Figure 8.6 *Loading performance of the app*

two very similar devices. On the first device you should keep the old version of the app while installing the update on the other device. Then you can compare the performance of the described section as well as the loading times to see if there is an improvement (see Figure 8.6).

Login and Payment

If your app provides a login feature or mobile payment process, it is critical that those features work. If your users can't log in or buy anything, you will lose money and harm your reputation. Features critical to your app must work to the maximum possible extent, so you need to be sure that they're well tested and covered by test automation. Take a look at the screenshot in Figure 8.7, where you can see that the mobile app provider had an issue with its subscription model.

Permissions

As I mentioned in Chapter 4, "How to Test Mobile Apps," it's very important that you use only the mobile app permissions you really need for your features to work. If you use permissions that users don't understand or that aren't required (see Figure 8.8), you will probably get lots of bad reviews in the stores, and it may even negatively impact your app's security. Be sure to check the permissions again before releasing your app.

Figure 8.7 *Checkout problems with premium subscription*

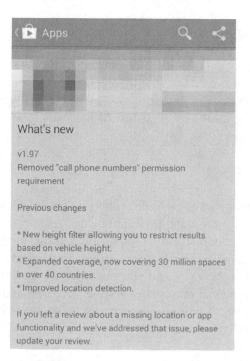

Figure 8.8 *Using permissions that aren't required*

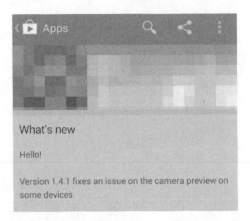

Figure 8.9 *Camera preview not working properly*

Mobile Device Hardware Usage

If your app uses mobile-device-specific hardware features such as the camera, be sure that the feature works on as many devices as possible. As you can see in Figure 8.9, the app provider had an issue with the camera preview on some devices. Testing for hardware support on different devices is a good task for crowd testers.

Since coming up with the idea of checking app update texts, I have continued doing this every time before I update to a newer version of an app. This is sometimes time-consuming and frustrating when I'm unable to reproduce the described bug, but it helped me a lot in improving my mobile testing skills. Just by reading through the app descriptions I learned so many new ways of generating mobile testing ideas as well as lots of new ways to provoke bugs during my daily testing work.

Observe

Another way to improve your mobile skills is by observing other people. Watch other people while they're using their mobile devices. Try to observe other people when among the public, for example, on a train, in the supermarket, or anywhere they're using an app. It is very interesting to see how other people use apps in totally different ways, and you can learn all sorts of things from your observations that you can reuse while testing your app and planning new features with your team. It will also help you to generate new testing ideas and bear other usage behaviors in mind.

> **Important**   Don't be too obvious and don't start stalking people while observing them.

During my observations I have noticed that many people don't know that a navigation drawer can be opened by swiping from the left of the screen to the right. They touch the navigation icon in the top left-hand corner to open it. I realized that not everyone is familiar with every feature that a mobile device or app has to offer. You should therefore take the time to observe other people in the wild or in test labs to see how they use their apps and then apply this knowledge in your mobile development process.

As a starting point I recommend that you observe either your colleagues or your family. This way you'll learn a lot, and they probably won't mind you observing them.

Take Part in Competitions and Test Cycles

If you're interested in competing with other software testers from around the world and learning from their testing experience, I recommend that you take part in a testing competition. There are lots of competitions throughout the year where software testers can register either as a team or alone to test a piece of software in different categories. The great thing about competitions is that you can share your knowledge and learn from other software testers. It's also fun to compete with other software testers to see how good your testing skills are compared to theirs.

I generally attend testing competitions in order to learn. I don't care about my final competition ranking; I just want to learn and improve my testing skills. I really like to see other testers during their work and pick up new testing ideas.

Here are a couple of testing competitions:

- Software Testing World Cup (www.softwaretestingworldcup.com/)
- Testathon (http://testathon.co/)

Another nice way to improve your testing skills and contribute to the testing community is Weekend Testing.[6] Weekend Testing is a platform where software testers can collaborate and learn from the testing community. As the name suggests, Weekend Testing takes place on the weekend and is all about testing software from different perspectives and sharing your testing work with other software testers. Have a look at the Weekend Testing Web site to check out the upcoming testing dates.

As mentioned in Chapter 6, "Additional Mobile Testing Methods," crowd testing is a software testing approach where you add software testers from all over the world to your in-house testing efforts. However, crowd testing can

---

6. http://weekendtesting.com/

serve another purpose as well: Registering as a crowd tester and attending testing cycles is a great way to learn as you get to see other mobile apps, the problems the app provider faces, and the bugs that come up. Furthermore, it is very interesting to see if your bug reports are good enough to be accepted by the crowd testing provider and mobile app provider.

> **Important**   Take part in testing competitions, share your knowledge with other software testers, and register with crowd testing platforms to see how other mobile apps work. Remember: While it may be interesting to see if your bug reports are accepted by the provider, your focus should be on improving your mobile testing skills.

The Mobile Community and the Mobile World

As mentioned in the previous section, learning from other software testers and mobile testers is a great way to improve your own mobile testing skills. I therefore recommend that you become an active part of the mobile community, for example, by registering on software testing platforms like Software Testing Club.[7]

Every software testing platform also has a mobile section where you can exchange news and views with other mobile testers. It's also very useful to join mobile testing groups on various social media platforms. There are always lots of great mobile developers and testers who want to interact on a certain topic or who have a problem. Helping someone with a problem is a great way to contribute to the mobile community. And don't be shy about asking questions even if you think they might be silly. There's no such thing as a stupid question!

If you don't have a Twitter account yet, I highly recommend that you create one. Every software testing and mobile testing expert uses Twitter to write about new testing ideas, blog posts, and other important information that is bound to help you during your daily working life. Most mobile testing experts also blog, so you should subscribe to their updates to get the latest information from them. In the next section I will list a few blogs and books that may be of interest to you.

Testing events and conferences are another way of exchanging with the mobile community. Lots of software testing conferences are hosted all over the world where software testing and mobile testing experts meet and share their knowledge in the form of talks or workshops. If you have the opportunity to do so, I highly recommend that you attend some conferences and meet other mobile testers in person to talk about a range of topics. You can also check to

---

7. www.softwaretestingclub.com/

see if there are any testing user groups in your area; these are generally free to attend and a great opportunity to meet other software testers nearby.

If you work in the mobile testing business, you could start blogging to keep a record of your experience and contribute to the mobile community. You can help other mobile testers with your acquired knowledge or blog about your experiences while becoming a mobile tester.

Besides learning from other mobile testers, it's very important that you stay up-to-date with regard to the latest technologies and features of the mobile operating systems and devices. You need to know when the different mobile device manufacturers release new devices and new versions of their operating systems. For a complete overview of such features, I recommend that you watch the keynote videos posted by the major manufacturers.

I also recommend that you use as many apps as possible from a range of different categories so you always have an overview of possible new features as well as new ways to implement and use an app.

Valuable Sources

This section of the chapter provides you with some interesting software testing communities, books, magazines, and blogs that you can use to improve your knowledge.

> **Important** These lists are by no means complete.

Conferences

The following conferences are worth going to:

- Agile Testing Days (www.agiletestingdays.com/)
- Belgium Testing Days (http://btdconf.com/)
- Dutch Testing Day (www.testdag.nl/)
- EuroSTAR (www.eurostarconferences.com/)
- Google Test Automation Conference (https://developers.google.com/google-test-automation-conference/)
- Iqnite (www.iqnite-conferences.com/index.aspx)
- Let's Test (http://lets-test.com/)
- Mobile App Europe (http://mobileappeurope.com/)
- Øredev (http://oredev.org/)

- STAREAST (http://stareast.techwell.com/)
- STARWEST (http://starwest.techwell.com/)
- TestBash (www.ministryoftesting.com/training-events/testbash/)
- TestExpo (http://testexpo.co.uk/)

Communities
The following software testing communities are worth looking into:

- Association for Software Testing (www.associationforsoftwaretesting.org/)
- Mobile QA Zone (www.mobileqazone.com/)
- Software Testing Club (www.softwaretestingclub.com)
- Testing Circus (www.testingcircus.com/)
- uTest community (www.utest.com)

Books
The following books are worth reading. Not all of them are about mobile testing, but they are an excellent source of knowledge for software testers.

- *Agile Testing* (http://lisacrispin.com/agile-testing-book-is-now-out/) by Lisa Crispin and Janet Gregory
- *Beautiful Testing* (www.amazon.com/gp/product/0596159811?tag=sw-testing-books-20) edited by Tim Riley and Adam Goucher
- *Explore It!* (http://pragprog.com/book/ehxta/explore-it) by Elisabeth Hendrickson
- *How Google Tests Software* (http://books.google.de/books?id=VrAx1ATf-RoC) by James A. Whittaker, Jason Arbon, and Jeff Carollo
- *Lessons Learned in Software Testing* (www.amazon.com/gp/product/0471081124?tag=sw-testing-books-20) by Cem Kaner, James Bach, and Bret Pettichord
- *Specification by Example* (http://specificationbyexample.com/) by Gojko Adzic
- *Tap into Mobile Application Testing* (https://leanpub.com/testmobileapps) by Jonathan Kohl

Magazines

The following magazines provide great content from experts in various industries. These magazines focus on specific software and mobile testing topics.

- *Agile Record* (www.agilerecord.com/)
- *Professional Tester* (www.professionaltester.com/magazine/)
- *Tea-time with Testers* (www.teatimewithtesters.com/)
- *Testing Circus* (www.testingcircus.com/)

Blogs

The following list contains great blogs from software testing experts:

- Gojko Adzic, http://gojko.net/
- James Bach, www.satisfice.com/blog/
- Michael Bolton, www.developsense.com/blog/
- Lisa Crispin, http://lisacrispin.com/
- Martin Fowler, http://martinfowler.com/
- Markus Gärtner, http://blog.shino.de/
- Shmuel Gershon, http://testing.gershon.info/
- Andy Glover, http://cartoontester.blogspot.co.uk/
- Adam Goucher, http://adam.goucher.ca/
- Elisabeth Hendrickson, http://testobsessed.com/
- Jim Holmes, http://frazzleddad.blogspot.com/
- Lena Houser, http://trancecyberiantester.blogspot.com/
- Eric Jacobson, www.testthisblog.com/
- Stephen Janaway, http://stephenjanaway.co.uk/stephenjanaway/blog/
- Viktor Johansson, http://therollingtester.com/
- Jonathan Kohl, www.kohl.ca/blog/
- Rob Lambert, http://thesocialtester.co.uk/
- Alan Page, http://angryweasel.com/blog/
- Huib Schoots, www.huibschoots.nl/wordpress/
- Rosie Sherry, www.rosiesherry.com/

The following blogs have multiple contributors:

- http://blog.inthewildtesting.com/
- http://blog.utest.com/ (uTest employees)
- http://googletesting.blogspot.de/ (Google employees)
- www.ministryoftesting.com/testing-feeds/ (a great testing feed collection)
- http://mobileapptesting.com/
- http://webapptesting.com/

And then there's my blog:

- www.adventuresinqa.com

Summary

Chapter 8 was all about skills and the required skill set of a mobile tester. Hiring mobile testers is not easy, because they are very rare. If you have found someone who could fit your company and position, be sure he or she has the following soft skills in order to be successful in the role of mobile tester:

- Communication
- Curiosity
- Critical thinking
- Tenacity
- Constant learner
- Creativity
- Customer focus
- Programming and technical skills

If you are a mobile tester and want to improve your testing skills, this chapter provided some suggestions. With lots of examples, the section "Learn from Other Apps" showed you how to improve your testing skills by trying to reproduce bugs in existing apps. In addition, it is important to be active in the mobile testing community, to learn from other mobile testers and to share your knowledge. At the end of the chapter an overview of important conferences, books, blogs, and magazines was provided.

Chapter 9

What's Next? And Final Thoughts

Welcome to the final chapter of this book! This chapter deals with the question "What's next?"

What's the next big thing mobile testers are going to have to deal with? What kinds of new technology are already out there, are on their way, or could arrive in the future? Are there any new testing challenges that we need to handle? Are there any new testing tools and test environments on the horizon?

To answer those questions, the following sections of this chapter describe some new technologies that are already on the market or due to arrive in the near future. To keep pace in the fast-growing world of technology, it's important for you to know what's in the pipeline.

The following sections can be used for further investigations and research if needed. No one is able to predict the future, but I'm convinced that the following technologies will become more and more important for mobile testers in the next couple of years.

Internet of Things

The Internet of Things (IoT) refers to the interconnection of uniquely identifiable embedded computing devices within the existing Internet infrastructure to offer different kinds of services. Things in the IoT can include a wide variety of devices such as human medical implants, biochips for animals, and cars with built-in sensors that communicate with one another to exchange information about the current traffic situation or provide drivers with certain information about their cars. There are also devices such as washing or coffee machines that can connect to the Internet so you can monitor them remotely. Everything that can be assigned an IP address and has the ability to provide and transfer data over a network is a thing in the IoT.

According to a study conducted by Gartner,[1] there will be up to 26 billion devices on the Internet of Things by 2020. And that figure doesn't include computers, tablets, or smartphones, which will reach the 7.3 billion mark by 2020. If you compare those numbers, IoT devices will dwarf all the existing smart devices. This will of course give rise to a whole new industry with people trying to connect everything to the Internet.

Here are some possible usage areas and scenarios for IoT:

- **Environmental monitoring:** Sensors can be used to monitor water quality, soil conditions, or the atmosphere.

- **Infrastructure management:** Bridges, railway tracks, and wind farms can be monitored.

- **Energy management:** Industrial manufacturers can optimize energy levels in real time.

- **Medical and health care systems:** People's health can be monitored remotely.

- **Building and home automation:** Alarm and heating systems can be monitored and managed.

- **Transport systems:** Cars can communicate with one another, such as to avoid traffic.

In order to standardize the IoT, a consortium[2] of companies has been formed to push along the IoT and develop default communication strategies, interfaces, and protocols. The following two sections provide some examples of current IoT devices and scenarios from different manufacturers.

Connected Home

Mobile device manufacturers Google and Apple are currently building their first IoT services and products which will form part of the IoT family alongside several other companies. In 2014, Google bought Nest Labs,[3] which builds intelligent thermostats and smoke alarms for smart homes. The thermostats

---

1. www.gartner.com/newsroom/id/2636073
2. www.openinterconnect.org/
3. https://nest.com/

and smoke alarms are connected to a Wi-Fi network and can be accessed from anywhere in the world using a computer, tablet, or smartphone.

Google is currently developing mobile apps for different mobile platforms that grant access to connected devices around the home. The product is intelligent as it can learn from user habits to control the heating system based on the time of day and the current month and determine whether or not the user is at home. Users can also define various scenarios to control their entire home heating system based on their needs. Because the devices are connected to the Internet, it's easy to auto-update them with new software versions including bug fixes and features.

Apple has introduced HomeKit[4] with iOS 8, which provides a framework to communicate and control connected devices in the user's home. Users will be able to automate and control IoT devices with their voice by using Siri. HomeKit will be able to control devices such as thermostats, lighting, doors, and other elements that can connect to the Internet. Apple provides the development framework for HomeKit and is currently looking for industry partners who want to implement Apple's HomeKit accessory protocol to be controlled by the HomeKit app.

As you can see, connected homes are already available on the market and enable entirely new ways of interacting with devices and parts of our daily life. There are plenty of potential new test scenarios, test environments, and testing challenges that are totally different from traditional testing or mobile testing.

> **Important**   Besides Google and Apple, there are a lot of other companies that are investing in and already have solutions in place for connected homes. I opted to write about Google and Apple because they also provide APIs for developers that allow them to build mobile applications around the connected home technology.

Connected Car

Connected cars are the next IoT example. Again, Google and Apple are already on their way to integrating the Android and iOS mobile operating systems into cars to make them even more intelligent. Google has introduced Android Auto,[5] and Apple released CarPlay.[6] Both Google and Apple will provide a lightweight version of their mobile operating systems to provide users with features they can use while driving, such as navigation, music, contacts, phone, and messages.

---

4. https://developer.apple.com/homekit/
5. www.android.com/auto/
6. www.apple.com/ios/carplay/

Besides their own mobile apps, both Google and Apple offer the option to use installed third-party apps in cars. There are already lots of car manufacturers that support both systems and let buyers choose the system they prefer.

However, using mobile apps with car displays gives rise to some new challenges for anyone involved in the software development process. For example, the provided apps and features shouldn't distract the driver and need to offer a very simple user interface with less information compared to mobile apps or Web applications.

The following four points must be considered when developing and testing mobile apps or other applications for connected cars:

- **Simple interface:** Car applications and interfaces should not distract the driver. The UI elements must be easy to use while the driver is at the wheel. Traditional input methods need to be reconsidered and should also include voice control.

- **Avoid useless features:** The feature set of an app required while driving is probably a lot smaller than for an app used on a smartphone. The app should therefore offer fewer features on the car display to prevent the driver from being overwhelmed or frustrated while at the wheel.

- **Third-party apps need guidelines:** Car manufacturers need to provide an API for third-party developers so their services can be integrated. However, this poses the challenge of creating very strict guidelines about what is and isn't possible.

- **Testing in the car:** Developing apps for cars is challenging enough in itself, but testing apps for cars is even more complex. It is simply not enough to test the app in a lab situation because cars are generally on the move, have different manufacturer years and models, and have lots of interfaces with other systems. Electronic interference in a car can have a huge impact on your app and the whole system. The provided app must be safe for the driver to use while at the wheel. Last but not least, the app must be well tested to avoid any critical bugs.

A good example of a connected car and IoT is the car manufacturer Tesla,[7] which builds cars that are completely connected to the Internet and can be partially controlled with the aid of a mobile app. The car receives automatic updates that improve features, fix bugs, and even solve problems with different parts of the engine. *Wired* magazine published an interesting article about Tesla as an example of IoT.[8]

---

7. www.teslamotors.com/
8. www.wired.com/2014/02/teslas-air-fix-best-example-yet-internet-things/

As you can see, the two examples—connected home and car—represent new challenges for the entire software development process. From a testing point of view in particular, these new technologies require different testing methods as well as new testing environments, new testing devices, and completely new testing scenarios.

Wearables

Wearable technology is a rapidly growing field that's expected to grow exponentially over the next few years. There are lots of new and innovative form factors for devices that can be worn on different parts of the body. These new form factors pose new challenges for companies as they look to find smart ways to make their product functional, usable, and lovable for their customers. The same applies to developers and software testers who need to rethink their work and the way they develop and test such products. Wearables generally involve smart watches, smart glasses, and fitness wristbands.

Smart Watches and Fitness Wristbands

Smart watches and fitness wristbands are extensions to mobile devices that send and receive information such as messages, news, incoming calls, and health status to and from mobile devices. To get the latest information from an app, users no longer need to take their device out of their pocket. Most devices can be controlled by the user's voice or a small touchscreen. However, a smart watch or fitness wristband is essentially useless without a mobile device to interact with.

The usability and design of smart watches and fitness wristbands need to be thoroughly tested and checked. Designing software for really small screens is not easy, which is why designers and UX experts need to rethink their concepts in order to build nice products that wearables users will love and use. Jonathan Kohl wrote an excellent article about his lessons learned when designing products for smart watches and wearables.[9]

If you have the opportunity to test wearables, especially smart watches or fitness wristbands, you should keep an eye on the look-and-feel of the device together with the software under test. This also includes testing the design and usability. When doing so, you should ask yourself the following questions to generate valuable feedback about the product:

- Is the device nice to wear?
- Does the app make sense on the wearable device?

---

9. www.kohl.ca/2014/lessons-learned-when-designing-products-for-smartwatches-wearables/

- Are the features easy to use and helpful?
- Do certain parts of the device get in the way while you're on the move and while you're using the software?
- How can the user interact with the smart watch or fitness wristband?

The look, feel, design, and usability are the main success factors when it comes to wearable technology. If a wearable device doesn't feel good, users will not buy or wear it.

From a technological point of view, testing smart watches has some additional challenges compared to mobile apps and devices. The fact that smart watches are extensions to mobile devices requires testing of the wearable device together with the software to see how both communicate with mobile devices in order to receive and transfer data. This scenario isn't something you can automate. I'm sure you're already aware of mobile device fragmentation, but this is compounded by the fact that smart watches and fitness wristbands need to work correctly within a different set of unique daily user scenarios, and all those scenarios require extensive in-the-wild testing. Such testing in a real-life environment will play an essential part in the success of software for smart watches.

Google introduced Android Wear[10] in 2014 to kick off the wearable device era. Apple introduced the Apple Watch[11] in September 2014 and started selling it in early 2015. If you search the Internet for smart watches and fitness wristbands, you'll come across various device manufacturers and all the different devices on the market.

For information about building software products for wearable devices, check out the Pebble developer,[12] the Google wearable,[13] and the Apple Watch[14] feature pages.

Smart Glasses

Google Glass is another wearable that was introduced by Google. Google Glass[15] includes almost the same hardware as a mobile device extended with an optical head-mounted display (OHMD) to have the content and information directly in front of your eyes. The glasses are equipped with lots of sensors and a camera to interact with your surroundings. You can control this wearable device with your voice or by using the touchpad on the side of the frame.

---

10. www.android.com/wear/
11. www.apple.com/watch/
12. https://developer.getpebble.com/
13. https://developer.android.com/training/building-wearables.html
14. www.apple.com/watch/features/
15. www.google.com/glass/start/

The explorer edition of Google Glass has been on sale in some countries since 2014, but lots of countries and companies have expressed privacy concerns since its introduction in 2012 because the device is able to record people in public without their permission. Furthermore, there are concerns about the product in terms of corporate secrets and safety considerations while using it in different scenarios, such as while driving a car or riding a motorbike.

However, Google provided a new way of using mobile technologies and set new standards and innovations in the world of wearable devices, even though the product isn't ready for the mass market yet. Google Glass is a great example of the direction technology will take over the coming years.

If you have the opportunity to develop and test software for smart glasses, don't forget to run through the list of questions applicable to smart watches. You'll also need to rethink your testing approach for this device.

Health Apps

Another interesting and growing market is mobile health apps. "The number of mHealth apps published on the two leading platforms, iOS and Android, have more than doubled in only 2.5 years to reach more than 100,000 apps (Q1 2014)" and ". . . will reach $26 billion in revenues by 2017, . . ." as quoted in the current mHealth App Developer Economics[16] report. This huge increase shows that mHealth apps will be on the rise in the near future.

The top four mHealth apps are:

1. **Fitness** apps (30%)

2. **Medical reference** apps (16%)

3. **Well-being** apps (15%)

4. **Nutrition** apps (8%)

The remainder of the mHealth apps are distributed among different categories such as medical condition management, diagnostics, compliance, reminders, alerts, and monitoring.

Health apps involve the use of mobile devices or wearables to monitor the human body for current blood pressure, pulse, heart rate, sleep patterns, calorie consumption, or current speed while running. The huge number of mHealth apps on the two leading platforms, iOS and Android, has convinced Apple and Google to invest in and develop mHealth APIs and apps for their mobile

---

16. http://mhealtheconomics.com/mhealth-developer-economics-report/

platforms. Apple introduced Health[17] for its customers and HealthKit[18] for its developers at the same time as it rolled out iOS 8. Google introduced Google Fit[19] in 2014. The fact that both Apple and Google are entering the health market will lead to several new devices and apps being rolled out in the near future.

As the numbers show, most of these apps help customers to track their fitness or dietary habits, but health apps also pose high risks to customers. Apps that manage insulin doses for patients with diabetes could have disastrous consequences if a bug occurs. This risk raises an important question: Can we trust health care apps?

Medical devices are generally regulated by the United States Food and Drug Administration (FDA), but this is not the case with every mobile health app. Experts from the *New England Journal of Medicine*[20] say that the FDA doesn't have enough resources to regulate all the health apps available in the different mobile app stores. Another challenge that is nearly impossible for the FDA and app providers to handle is all the mobile operating system updates provided by the different vendors. Each mobile platform receives more than one or two updates a year, and each operating system update must be compliant with the FDA regulations.

So the answer to the previous question is **no**. We can't trust health apps if they aren't regulated by any institution because we can't be sure that the delivered data is correct and free of mistakes.

If you have the opportunity to test mobile health and fitness apps, please bear the following points in mind:

- Get information from the FDA and other medical institutions with regard to regulations and health care workflows.

- The provided data *must* be correct in order to protect human life.

- Data security is a very important aspect due to the privacy of a person's state of health.

- Mobile health apps must have excellent usability in order to cover the target group's needs.

- Geolocation data must be correct for fitness trackers.

Besides that, all of the mobile testing knowledge you have acquired in this book also applies to health and fitness apps.

---

17. www.apple.com/ios/whats-new/health/
18. https://developer.apple.com/healthkit/
19. https://developers.google.com/fit/
20. www.nejm.org/doi/full/10.1056/NEJMhle1403384

If you'd like to find out more about mHealth, visit the *mHealthNews*[21] or mobile Health Economics[22] Web sites or have a look at the mHealth App Developer Economics 2014 study.[23]

Final Thoughts

This is the last section of my book about mobile testing, and I'd like to provide you with some final thoughts. During the course of this book you've learned a great deal about mobile devices, mobile apps, mobile users, and the tools that are important when it comes to mobile testing. I also hope you've learned from my ideas and experiences during my time as a mobile tester.

This book is designed to help you in your daily life as a mobile tester, mobile developer, or product manager by giving you the impetus to generate new testing ideas and try out new mobile testing approaches. It should also serve as a basis for developing your own testing ideas and approaches, while also helping you to extend your knowledge level.

As you have seen, the mobile development and testing business is rapidly changing with lots of new technology entering the market every day and plenty more in the pipeline. This is why it's important that you stay up-to-date, strive to learn constantly, and adapt your skills to the ever-changing world of technology.

Five Key Success Factors

To round things off, I'd like to provide you with my five key success factors for becoming a successful mobile tester.

Success Factor 1: Have High Expectations

Mobile users have high expectations, and you should also have very high expectations when it comes to mobile apps and their usability, performance, and feature set. Bear in mind that mobile customers will uninstall your app very quickly if they're not happy with it, and they'll probably submit a bad review to the app store. It's therefore important that you always keep your customers in mind, encourage good usability and performance, and make sure that all the important bugs get fixed. Keep the KIFSU principle in mind and listen to your customers' needs.

---

21. www.mhealthnews.com/
22. http://mhealtheconomics.com/
23. http://mhealtheconomics.com/mhealth-developer-economics-report/

Success Factor 2: Be an Expert on Mobile Devices

A successful mobile tester needs to be an expert on mobile devices. It is essential to know all the different hardware and software features of mobile devices from the various platforms. This knowledge will help you to keep lots of different test scenarios in mind during your daily business. If you're able to do so, buy mobile devices using the different platforms so you can stay up-to-date. If buying is not an option, try to rent them from a mobile device lab.

You should also subscribe to various technology blogs and news pages in order to get the latest news about mobile operating systems and mobile devices. I recommend that you watch the keynote videos of the major mobile manufacturers to find out the latest information about the different platforms.

Success Factor 3: Be on the Move

One of the most important points you should bear in mind when testing a mobile app is to be on the move while you're testing. Your customers use their mobile apps in many different scenarios, locations, and data networks. Therefore, it's essential that you test your app in several data networks with different network speeds to replicate real-life scenarios. While testing your app in the wild, you'll doubtless come across lots of different problems that would probably never show up in the office. When testing an app on the move, there will be lots of interferences that could have an impact on your app when using the various sensors and interfaces a mobile device has on offer.

So grab a bag, fill it with mobile devices, and start testing in the wild right now!

Success Factor 4: Build Up Your Programming Skills

Mobile testers need to be able to write test automation code. If you don't have any programming skills right now, do your best to get into programming so you can write reliable and robust test automation scripts for your mobile app. Programming skills will also help you support the developers with their regression tests, and you'll be able to communicate and discuss the app's code with the developers. If your programming skills need brushing up, now's the time to read some programming language books or run through some online tutorials.

Success Factor 5: Be a Constant Learner

The final success factor in becoming a better mobile tester is to be a constant learner. This doesn't just apply to mobile testers; it should be the case for anyone involved in the IT business. The technologies used to build complex systems including mobile apps are changing constantly. Furthermore, new ways of using and communicating with new technologies are on their way, and it's important for you to find out about them as soon as possible.

Besides learning new technologies, you should also work on improving your testing skills. Great ways to do this include reading lots of blogs and books, attending conferences, and taking part in competitions to learn from other mobile testers and share experiences with them. This will help you to improve your testing ideas, approaches, and skills.

Don't shy away from trying out new things—make mistakes and learn from them.

Summary

The last chapter of this book covered the topic "What's next?" What are the upcoming technology trends software testers have to deal with? I described five possible technology trends that are already on the market or on their way. The five technologies are

- Internet of Things
- Connected homes
- Connected cars
- Wearables
- Health apps

In the "Final Thoughts" section I outlined five key success factors to become a successful mobile tester. Those success factors are

- Have high expectations.
- Be an expert on mobile devices.
- Be on the move.
- Build up your programming skills.
- Be a constant learner.

That's it; thank you very much for reading my book. I hope you learned a lot of new things and got new ideas for your daily life as a mobile tester.

Happy mobile testing!

Index